230, 1   10133

FASTING

FASTING
A Neglected Discipline

David R Smith

CHRISTIAN LITERATURE CRUSADE
Fort Washington, Pennsylvania 19034

© *David R. Smith, England 1954*

CHRISTIAN LITERATURE CRUSADE
Fort Washington, Pennsylvania 19034

CANADA
1440 Mackay Street, Montreal, Quebec

First Impression 1954
This American edition 1969
Sixth printing 1975

SBN 87508-515-6

Contents

'Fasting is a laudable practice, and we have reason to lament it, that it is so generally neglected among christians'

—Matthew Henry

'Christians who take heed unto their ways, and desire to walk humbly and closely with God, will find frequent occasion for private seasons of afflicting their souls before their Father which is in secret'

—John Wesley

'I wonder whether we have ever fasted? I wonder whether it has even occurred to us that we ought to be considering the question of fasting? The fact is, is it not, that this whole subject seems to have dropped right out of our lives, and right out of our whole christian thinking'

—D. Martyn Lloyd-Jones

'It was not Christ's intention to reject or despise fasting ... it was His intention to restore proper fasting'

—Martin Luther

Introduction

In the Preface to the first edition of this book, fifteen years ago, I pointed out that there was a dire need for a concise modern work on the subject of fasting, in view of the fact that the last recorded title dealing with this discipline was dated 1861. In the British Museum there are very few books which deal with this doctrine, and the best of these was first published in 1580! Only in commentaries and biblical dictionaries is there any clear mention of fasting, and even there, we do not find all the help that one would desire.

This sad lack of suitable literature on a subject, which is mentioned often in the Holy Scriptures, may account for the attention which this book has attracted. One would not think that a work on real discipline, with so obvious a title, would sell very well at all. However, the demand for copies of these pages has continued steadily since 1954, and shows no sign of lessening. In fact, now we have the book being published in several countries, and this is the latest American edition. We must assume that people are not only interested in the subject of personal discipline, but also are willing to consider personal sacrifice of the kind that our forefathers were ready to endure.

No part of this book has been written lightly; all of it is the result of studying the Scriptures, reading the opinions of countless saints, and personal experience. The theme is approached in a practical way, without any appeal to the emotions. The reader is not badgered into undertaking anything which will prove regrettable; extremism is not only avoided—it is condemned. As a result, these pages should appeal not only to the student, but also to the average christian who is seeking ways to a deeper experience. This book is intended for those who want to know Christ better, and who are willing for some personal inconvenience in that pilgrimage; they will discover here that fasting is a means to precious blessings.

Although I would hesitate to claim any inspiration of the following text (for understandable reasons), I was guided in divine ways to pen this manuscript, nevertheless. The last fifteen years have provided me with ample proof that God has seen fit to use it, worldwide, to the enrichment of many readers. The scriptural quotations are from the 1611 version of the English Bible, unless otherwise stated.

DAVID R. SMITH

London
June, 1969

I: The Discipline

'... they ministered unto the Lord and fasted ...'

It is quite common for christians to think of fasting in terms of self-denial which is wholly spiritual, and not to consider it as being connected, in any way, to the human body. This may be due to the fact that the subject of fasting is discussed in public only rarely, or it may be because we are tempted to separate our faith from all earthly experiences. Whatever the reason, it is true to say that fasting is not practised on a wide scale, and is understood very little. Considering the extent to which we read our Bibles, through the encouragement of various agencies, this lack of understanding and experience is strange, for the Holy Scriptures are full of references to this subject. Not only did the saints of the Old Testament fast regularly, but also the Apostles, and Our Lord Himself, adopted this form of personal denial. However, more than this; there is little doubt that fasting was common among the early christians, and that they were encouraged, both by precept and example, to continue this ancient discipline.

We must not be surprised that some people have suggested that fasting is no longer necessary to christian experience; these are days when many divergent statements are being made. A christian does not pay attention to the views of mere men, he studies God's Word in order to discover for himself what God expects of him. Neither must we be surprised if someone sets out to comprehend all that there is to know about fasting and becomes confused in the process; this discipline has been so perverted by fanatics, hypocrites, and formalists, that we have to separate the teaching which is divine from that which is human. This is the purpose of the book before you now; we shall seek to discover the true biblical doctrine.

WHAT IS FASTING?

Every christian has a sense of responsibility towards others and himself, as well as towards His Lord. There are duties to be performed—duties known inwardly and through reading the Bible—in connection with one's relationships with other christians, Almighty God, and oneself. Our Lord made this perfectly clear in the Sermon on the Mount, when He referred to three aspects of christian behaviour (Matthew 6:1–18). Almsgiving is one example of a duty which every believer has towards others, prayer is an example of a duty which he has towards God, and fasting is an example of one duty which he has towards himself. Of this last named discipline, Jesus said 'When you fast, be not—as the hypocrites—of a sad countenance: for they disfigure their faces, that they may appear unto men to fast. Verily I say unto you, they have their reward'. Whatever else may be said, at this stage, it is obvious that Our Lord did not forbid fasting; it would be more true to say that He presumed that His disciples would fast at some time in their christian lives, but that when they did so He wished that they do it correctly.

The word used by Jesus in this passage means 'not to eat'; therefore, a literal translation could be 'When you do not eat, be not . . .', but this would make no sense, for the cessation from eating had a religious meaning.

Whenever people abstain from food *on religious grounds*, the correct word to use as a description of their behaviour—is the word 'fast'. It would not be right to describe men on a hunger strike as *fasting*, unless the strike was in the context of a local church; similarly, for a body of people to stop eating—in public—in order to attract attention to a good cause is not *fasting*. 'To fast, is to abstain from food, as a religious observance' is the definition from the *Concise Oxford Dictionary*, and is typical of others.

It may be said, then, that fasting is essentially religious, but not essentially christian and involves the personal intake of food. Because it is not essentially christian, this discipline can be found in other religions, both ancient and modern. The disciples who heard Jesus say 'When you fast' would not be surprised by His words, for they had fasted before on many occasions; the Jewish faith provided for such times of self-discipline. John the Baptist practised, and also taught his disciples to practise, regular fasting.[1] The people of that time were used to the idea that all Jews fasted at least once a year,[2] and that the ones who were particularly religious did so more often than that. Almost all of the religious faiths known to modern man have, at times, announced days of fasting. Our Lord was not advocating something new by this remark of His about fasting; religion and fasting have gone together, in greater or smaller measure, from the beginning.

It must be admitted, however, that the discipline of fasting has been broadened out to such an extent, over the centuries, that the word is now used to describe activity which is not essentially religious. For example, one hears much about fasting in Nature Cure circles, where diet plays a large role in most of the remedies; fasting is undertaken for the sake of personal physical health and not for any religious reason. We must accept such a use of the word, even if we do not agree with it, because it has been established over a long period. Whilst it would be preferable if this activity were called 'health dieting', just as public political fasts might be called 'hunger strikes' or 'hunger protests', and *not* 'fasting', we have to accept the misusage of this word, as well as that of others. So, whilst we must contend that *fasting*, if the word is correctly used, is a religious activity in which the person concerned abstains from food for a pre-determined length of time, it must be acknowledged that people have used the word to describe other activity with a similar appearance.

OUTWARD AND INWARD FASTING

A notable author who took time to enlarge upon the subject of fasting was Thomas Cartwright, who was a distinguished Elizabethan Puritan and a leading non-conformist. He wrote *The Holy Exercise of a True Fast* in 1580, and in that volume showed the difference between religious fasting which involved the body only, and that which involves the mind and spirit, as well as the body. He said that true fasting consists of outward bodily exercises, together with 'inward virtues, helped forward by the bodily exercises'. Cartwright was the first minister in England, after the Reformation, to expound this matter so clearly, and by so doing he corrected some of the confused ideas about fasting which had circulated for centuries. There is all the difference in the world between mere dietary discipline, even if it is entered into with a view to being more religious, and spiritual self-denial, which is assisted by dietary discipline. As Paul said 'bodily exercise profiteth little: but godliness is profitable unto all things' (1 Timothy 4:8). Outward fasting without inward fasting, if entered into for religious purposes, is a form of godliness without any dynamic or benefit.

This does not mean that outward fasting only is of no value; clearly it plays an important role in Nature Cure remedies, and has proved invaluable in times of National crisis. When governmental leaders call a nation to a day of prayer and fasting, it cannot be conceived that every citizen will fast inwardly as well as outwardly; those who are religious will enter into the spirit of the occasion, but those who are irreligious can only perform that duty which they are able to embrace. The point is that all religious fasting has had the intention of being both outward and inward, and must—of necessity—embrace both these aspects, or else it is not fasting, in the proper sense of the word. It is obvious that fasting can be mis-used, prostituted, or completely mis-understood, and we shall consider such possibilities in due course, but it must be borne in mind always that fasting (as understood by the Jews, and as expounded by our Lord) involves the mind and the spirit, as well as the body, and is entered into only for religious reasons.

AFFLICTING THE SOUL

When the commandment 'And this shall be a statue for ever unto you, that in the seventh month, on the tenth day of the month, you shall afflict your souls, and do no work at all' went forth to the early Jews,[2] the word *fast* was not used; instead we see the phrase 'afflict your souls'. However, 'they all fasted on this day from food, except the sick and the children, and laid aside their ornaments'.[3] They did this because if we 'afflict our souls' we must involve our bodies in the act of denial, or else the exercise is partial only. 'This

13

afflicting of the soul withdrew the man from earthly joys; the world and its scenes faded away, while he contemplated his guilt and the wrath of his God, and then the atonement provided by God'.[4]

The phrase 'afflict the soul' seems old fashioned until it is interpreted by the use of modern words, but the activity has been normal for all those who have recognised their lost estate, and known that they were without hope unless God saved them. When Paul became aware of his true spiritual situation, on the Damascus road, 'he was three days without sight, and neither did eat nor drink'.[5] Similarly, Ahab rent his clothes, put on sackcloth, and fasted,[6] when he heard what the Lord planned to do with him, and David wept and chastened his soul with fasting,[7] when shame overcame him. If we 'afflict our souls' we humble ourselves in the presence of God; we are abased. There are times when Christians must take this kind of action, as James makes quite clear: 'Draw nigh to God, and He will draw nigh to you ... be afflicted, and mourn, and weep: let your laughter be turned to mourning, and your joy to heaviness. Humble yourselves in the sight of the Lord, and He shall lift you up' (James 4:8–10).

The Jews obeyed the commandment to fast on the tenth day of the seventh month, and so the annual day of sorrow and atonement became the 'most memorable day of the Jewish Year. It was the day of expiation for the sins of the whole people, and was observed as a perfect sabbath; it was the one fast-day of the Jewish calendar; it was emphatically *the day*.'[8] This fast was being observed by the Jews during the lifetime of the Apostles (Acts 27:9), and is so still, together with about twenty-two other added ones. Then, as now, 'afflicting the soul' involved a restraining of all activities which gave pleasure to the mind and body of the person concerned; the

14

expression implies 'the sacrifice of the personal will, which gives to fasting all its value'.[9]

TO FAST IS TO ABSTAIN

Having seen that the word *fast* means 'to abstain from food for religious reasons', we must now go on to consider what this entails. Does abstinence imply all food, or only some food? If one abstains from food, does this include drink also? In order to obtain the fullest answers to these questions it is necessary to devote more time and attention to the teaching of the Bible than to that of christians through the intervening centuries, since the discipline of fasting has suffered greatly from the writings of both fanatics and formalists.

The Old Testament word for *fast* means 'covering the mouth' and the New Testament word means 'not to eat'. This should be sufficient proof for most readers, but in order to establish the point, here are some authoritative definitions: '*Fast* is the word used for total or partial abstinence from food for a certain period';[10] 'To fast means to abstain from food, but the word must be understood as expressive of abstinence from food for a religious purpose, and in connection with, and in subservience to, religious exercises';[11] 'Fasting, in a religious sense, is a voluntary abstinence from food for a religious purpose. It is a natural expression of sorrow, because sorrow destroys the desire for food and the power to digest it. This abstinence is either total or partial, either for a day or for protracted periods';[12] 'Fasting is a religious abstinence from all comforts of this life ... first in an utter forbearing of all food ...';[13] 'In early times, fasting meant entire abstention from food';[14] 'This is so clear that it would be labour lost to quote the words of David, Nehemiah, Isaiah, and the prophets which followed, or of our Lord and His Apostles; all agreeing in this, that to fast is, not to eat for a time prescribed.'[15]

This does not mean, however, that we can only fast when we cease eating. The discipline, which is applied to oneself only, involving *food*, is an indication of our whole approach towards personal salvation; it reflects one's sense of discipleship and individual discipline. If a christian fasts, in a christian way, he is not just disciplining his eating—he is symbolising all of his personal life in one action. A christian who fasts is, by virtue of his new nature in Christ, an abstainer in all respects; he does not carry anything to excess and always knows when to draw the line—as far as his bodily appetites are concerned.

If the matter is still unclear, it is not difficult to compare the experiences of those who fasted in biblical times with our own view of the subject. If they were fasting in the correct way, they will show us what the discipline is, by example. The Psalmist wrote 'My knees are weak through fasting; and my flesh faileth of fatness' (Psalm 109:24), clearly indicating that his fasting involved his diet. Esther said to Mordecai 'Fast for me, and neither eat nor drink three days, night or day; I also and my maidens will fast likewise' (Esther 4:16), showing that their fast included bodily denial as well as personal sorrow. When Jesus fasted, just prior to the inauguration of His national ministry, 'He did eat nothing' (Luke 4:2) and 'He was afterward an hungred' (Matthew 4:2), leaving the matter in no doubt.

Why have so many christians read those words of Jesus 'When you fast' and yet not appreciated that they imply 'abstaining from food', or that the phrase involves themselves? It is possible to read verses repeatedly, but learn little, until one day—when we are desiring God's guidance —light dawns. On the other hand, many a christian has understood the meaning of these words, but not fully realised their importance, because local churches have ignored the subject. Hosts of godly people have sensed a personal lack here, but have not thought of fasting (in the way that the Scriptures propose it) because the word 'fast' has become vague to them. This is due partly to the fact that *mortification* has been confused with fasting. Since *mortification* acquired a bad name as a result of ascetic practices in the early christian centuries and the Dark Ages, it is only mentioned now in either High Church, or Calvinistic circles. Because *fasting* played such an important role in *ascetic mortification* (along with celibacy, flagellation, and monastic living), fasting today is considered to be practised only by extremists. Wthout realising it, we have put the word out of our christian vocabulary, and denied ourselves the knowledge of any experience of fasting. There is a true biblical *mortification*, by the power of the Holy Spirit (Romans 8:13), which is essential to New Testament holiness, and which may embrace fasting, but fasting is not essential to it.

When Jesus elucidated the implications of discipleship in, what is commonly called, the Sermon on the Mount, He made it perfectly clear that the christian life is demanding, even though it provides one with liberty. A selfish person is unable to enjoy the Gospel; a christian is someone who has begun to deny himself, and is in the continuous process of denying himself. Jesus said 'If any man will come after Me, let him deny himself, and take up his cross, and follow Me'.[16] Self-denial is not limited to one particular kind of giving; it embraces all personal disciplines. Fasting is only one discipline; nevertheless, it is self-denial. This does not mean that to fast is to embrace legalism; it is gospel liberty which encourages us to deny ourselves.

FASTING IS SELF-DENIAL

Self-denial is important to the christian life, because it is character-forming. Self-denial encourages a believer to see the Lord as his all-in-all and his complete source of sufficiency. The christian who denies himself becomes less important, in his own eyes, and grows into an awareness of the glorious sovereignty of God. As self grows less and less, Jesus becomes more and more of a personal Saviour and King. Jesus did not offer His followers a feather-bed life;[17] He made the need for personal discipline perfectly clear. We are called to live a consistent life of self-effacement and unselfishness. We may have inherited eternal life —that gift which God bestows; we may be saved from sin by grace—the way having been clearly marked and open for us; but to enrich that salvation, continually growing in grace, there must be self-denial. To go on with the Lord means to live in obedience; in order to be enlarged in one's spiritual life we must desire the continual death of self. No christian can become victorious and useful if he ignores personal discipline. Although Grace is the key to all christian victory, and whilst we must not forget that we have victory by grace through faith, the discipline of the individual life is only ignored at the peril of the individual soul.

FASTING AND PARTIAL FASTING

For reasons which may never be fully understood, christians have often sought to nullify the exact meaning of the word *fast*, down through the centuries. Instead of accepting the fact that fasting involves the appetite and requires no intake of food, excuses have been made, with the result that the discipline has been ignored, explained away, or diluted. This behaviour has caused theologians to explain the differences between the variations that exist in the biblical record concerning fasting, in the light of more modern tendencies, and to give each category a name. For example, it has been said that if one ceases eating for a period covering three or more meals, then one is truly fasting. However, if one misses only one meal, or cuts down on

18

the amount eaten, the discipline is better described as *abstinence*. Others have sought to set apart the biblical fasting already fully considered by giving the word adjectives, such as 'true fasting'[18] and 'real fasting'.[19] This seems to be unnecessary if christians uphold the meaning of the word *fast*; certainly, we shall need a new adjective each century if we are not careful.

Having seen that fasting means *not eating*, we have every right to ask if it can ever be partial and remain *fasting*, in the biblical sense of the word. This is a wise question in view of the way that this discipline has been prostituted at times. For example, Martin Luther wrote: 'I really dare say that in what they termed *fasting* in the papacy, I never saw a genuine fast. How can I call it a fast if someone prepares a lunch of expensive fish, with the choicest spices, more and better than for two or three other meals, and washes it down with the strongest drink, and spends an hour or three at filling the stomach until it is stuffed? Yet that was the usual thing even among the very strictest monks. Therefore, I say that never, in my whole life, have I seen a fast in the entire papacy that was really a christian fast.'[20] On the other hand, we must not allow extremism to force our hand, since partial fasting has a place in the Scriptures.

When Abraham's servant arrived at the home of Laban, at the end of a tiring journey, he announced that he would not eat until he had explained the reason for his errand (Genesis 24:33); this was not a fast in the full sense of the word, but it was self-denial for religious reasons. When David heard of the death of Saul and Jonathan he, together with his men, mourned and wept, and fasted until evening (2 Samuel 1:12); this was no 24-hour vigil which had been pre-meditated—it seems to have been more of a national sadness than godly sorrow—but it is called a fast. Then, again, when Daniel decided that he would not defile himself with the king's meat and wine, he asked if he and his friends might have a herbal diet for ten days, and only water to drink (Daniel 1:8–20); this was not fasting altogether, but it was fasting in part, for the spiritual fasting that went with this dietary discipline was just as real as when Daniel stopped eating completely, at other times in his life.[21]

It may be said, therefore, that although fasting usually implies that the christian will miss at least three meals completely, we must be willing for people to use the word for partial fasting only. However, it would be better if christians used the words, *fasting*, *partial fasting*, and *abstinence* correctly. For the remainder of this book, this practice will be adopted.

FASTING WITHOUT WATER

We have seen that fasting is connected with eating; so far, we have made no reference to the part played by *drinking* in this discipline; this is because we shall consider the *way* in which christians fast in chapter six. However, due to the fact that there are several references in the Bible to people who fasted *without water*, we must now deal with this aspect. The first case is quoted in Exodus 34:28, where we read that Moses was on Mount Sinai for 'forty days and forty nights; he did neither eat bread nor drink water'; this experience is also related by Moses in Deuteronomy 9:9. The next case can be found in Ezra 10:6, where we read that Ezra did 'eat no bread, nor drink water'; next, in Esther 4:16 we see that Esther said to Mordecai 'fast for me, and neither eat nor drink three days, night or day'; finally, in Acts 9:9 we learn that Paul 'was three days without sight, and did neither eat nor drink'. Whilst it may be said that only four illustrations, in the whole biblical record prove no rule, it is obvious that there have been times when men have found it necessary to fast in this extreme way. The word *extreme* is quite proper here, since we have no reference to a drinking self-denial in any of the other long fasts of famous saints, or of our Lord. When Jesus finished His forty day fast, it is recorded that 'He was hungry' and that during the fast 'He ate nothing'— there is no mention of Him being 'thirsty' or 'drinking nothing'.

Therefore, it may be said that although God might call some of His people to the extreme fast of going without both food and water, and will sustain them miraculously in such circumstances, this is not the usual implication in ordinary fasting, and should be avoided if possible. This practice will be called *extreme fasting*, for the remainder of this book.

IS FASTING COMMANDED?

Thomas Cartwright wrote that 'fasting is an abstinence *commanded* of the Lord, to make solemn profession of our repentance'.[22] On the other hand, John Brown wrote that Christ did *not command* these exercises, 'but proceeded on the principle that the children of the kingdom would perform them'.[23] These two opinions reflect the views of reformed theologians, who have believed in the discipline of fasting; either it has been said that fasting is commanded, or else that it is recommended only. Since these divergent opinions are both based upon the biblical evidence for fasting, we will consider this now. The verses which have been quoted as saying that fasting is *commanded* are:

1. Leviticus 16:29–31, where the words 'a statute for ever' are used. Cartwright insisted that the Jewish annual fast on the Day of Atonement should be observed by christians, as an annual day of personal humbling, despite the advent of Christ with His Gospel promises; he does not, however, have many allies. Perhaps it seemed vital

21

for him to stress the need for at least one day of fasting among christians, in his particular historic situation, but there is little doubt that he over-stressed the point. There is no record of Jesus, the Apostles, or Paul, exhorting believers to maintain this annual fast, as though it was obligatory. In fact, fasting is not mentioned in the apostolic list of necessary things in Acts 15:13–29. This does not mean that personal 'afflicting of the soul' is out of date, for—as Matthew Henry wrote—'By repentance we must afflict our souls, not only fasting for a time from the delights of the body, but inwardly sorrowing for our sins, and living a life of self-denial and mortification.'[24] Such sorrow for sin must be for as long as man lives a human fallen life, but this is not the same as obeying a command to fast on specified occasions.

2. In Matthew 4:1–4, Mark 1:12–13, and Luke 4:1–4, we are told that our Lord fasted for forty days. In 1 Peter 2:21, we are told that Christ is our Example, and so—it is said—we must fast in the way that He did. This must be dismissed as extremism, for the teaching of Peter, at this point in his Epistle, is not connected with personal discipline, but with persecution and trials.

3. In Matthew 17:21, Jesus said that 'this kind goeth not out but by prayer and fasting', as though fasting was an essential feature of christian life. Only a fanatic for fasting would base a doctrine for personal self-denial upon words which allude to the casting out of demons, or a preparation for christian service. Also, the word *fast* does not appear in this verse in the most reliable ancient manuscripts.

4. In Acts 14:23 there is a suggestion that the setting apart of christians for service should be attended with fasting. This may well be the case, but it proves nothing about the use of fasting as a private discipline which has been *commanded*. We must differentiate between personal

behaviour and congregational behaviour. However, this idea that all ordination (or similar) services must be accompanied by fasting is not borne out in other places in the same book in the Bible. That the early christians fasted together sometimes, is clear, but that it was obligatory is far from clear.

5. In Matthew 9:14-15 and Luke 5:33-35, our Lord said that His disciples could hardly fast when He was with them, but that they would fast 'when the bridegroom shall be taken away'. The challenge of these verses is inescapable, since it is impossible to assume that these words mean only that the disciples were to fast after the Crucifixion, but not at all after the Ascension. There is plenty of evidence that the disciples were *sorrowful* immediately following the Crucifixion, but there is no record of them *fasting*. In fact, to look at it from the opposite point of view, we have more than one record of them fasting long *after* the Ascension. If Christ, in these verses, commanded the disciples to cease fasting after His Ascension, they clearly disobeyed Him. Christ can only have meant that christian people are unable to fast when He is with them in Person, but sometimes need to fast when He is not with them in Person, even though He is within them by the Holy Spirit. Nevertheless, only a brave theologian would dare to assert that these words constitute a *command*. They do make it plain that Christ both upheld the discipline and anticipated that christians would fast, but they cannot be said to state that every christian must fast either on the Jewish Fast Days, or any other day.

IS FASTING A DUTY?

So then, although the Jews were commanded to fast in Old Testament times, in a prescribed manner, there is no similar command to christians; that early law was but a type of that which was to be written on the hearts of believers, after they had experienced the New Birth. However, although fasting is not commanded in the New Testament, it is a duty which christians do perform. A command is an *order*, whilst a duty is an *expression of respect*. Christians do not fast simply because they have been told to do so (although this may happen in the case of local church fasts, or civic fasts), but because it is one natural outcome of their discipleship—they fast for the same reason that they pray. In Matthew 6:1–18, Jesus embraced fasting with both prayer and alms-giving, and introduced each subject by the use of the same words: 'When you...' 'Fasting is a duty required of the disciples of Christ, when God—in His providence—calls to it, and when the case of their own souls—upon any account—requires it.... However, it is not so much a duty for its own sake, as a means to dispose us for other duties.'[25] It seems that there, 'quite clearly, is implicit teaching of, and almost an advocacy of fasting... It was something that was regarded by our Lord as right and good for christian people.'[26] 'Many of us are blameable in having left altogether untried, a means of giving greater intenseness to our attention, and greater fervour to our devotion, which nature seems to dictate.'[27]

When a man is born of the Spirit of God and adopted into the Heavenly family, he finds himself completely surrounded, and securely protected, by the ever-lasting arms of God. This environment, even in adverse conditions, draws a more than natural response from the heart of the christian. As believers seek God and search after deeper fellowship, so there dawns upon them the need to live in such a way that they glorify the Lord. Peter, John and the other disciples, loved Jesus; they had reason to do; He had become their Lord and Master, and they were willing to die for His sake. They realised how deep His love for them

24

was; it drew the best out of them. In such circumstances, the Lord spoke to them about praying and giving. Following this counsel, He said 'When you fast . . .' He did not declare 'You've got to fast'; He offered advice with picked words, and yet as though it came into His mind in passing: by the way, '*when you* fast. . . .' To the disciple who is seeking a closer walk, and to those who desire more of the life of the Spirit of God in them, this is a drawing word.

DEFINITION

Having sought to explain the nature of this neglected discipline, we now need a contemporary definition:

Fasting is an age-old practice, common in most religions, which involves the cessation of eating for an agreed time, but requires the drinking of water at least, unless extreme circumstances demand otherwise. This practice was commanded by God in Old Testament times, in order that men might have an annual reminder of their sinful nature, and was assumed, by Jesus, to be a spiritual duty to which believers would sometimes resort. When practised by christians, there is no ulterior motive, since the glory of God alone is the object in view; to a christian, fasting involves the whole man and symbolises total discipline. Except on special civic, or local church, days of penitence, christian fasting is—of necessity—private and secret. To the christian, fasting is not a ritual, to be indulged in regularly, but a source of intimate delight, even though it may involve heart searching and sorrow; for the value of this discipline lies not in its immediate effect, but in the results which flow from its practice, and in the gradual effect which it has upon the individual believer.

NOTES

[1] Luke 5:33
[2] Leviticus 16:29–31, 23:26–32 and Numbers 29:7
[3] From Matthew Henry's comments on these verses

4 Andrew Bonar: *Leviticus:* p. 417
5 Acts 9:9
6 1 Kings 21:27–29
7 Psalm 69:10
8 Farrar's *Early Days of Christianity:* vol. 1, p. 431
9 Unger's *Bible Dictionary:* p. 345
10 P. R. B. Barker: *Chambers's Encyclopaedia:* under Fasting
11 John Brown: *Discourses and Sayings:* p. 255
12 Charles Hodge: *Princeton Sermons:* p. 262
13 Thomas Cartwright: *The Holy Exercise of a True Fast*
14 *Oxford Dictionary of the Christian Church:* under Fasting
15 John Wesley: *Sermon on Fasting:* 22–1–1
16 Matthew 16:24
17 John 6:60–66
18 Thomas Cartwright's phrase
19 The phrase used by Hermas
20 *Luther's Works:* comments on Matthew 6:16–18
21 Daniel 9:3, for example
22 In Cartwright's *The Holy Exercise of a True Fast*
23 *Discourses and Sayings:* p. 255
24 Part of Henry's comments on Leviticus 16
25 Part of Henry's comments on Matthew 6:16–18
26 Dr. D. Martyn Lloyd-Jones: *Studies in the Sermon on the Mount:* p. 36
27 John Brown: *Discourses and Sayings:* p. 258

II: The Purpose

'. . . fast not unto men, but unto thy Father . . .'

Almost everything that we do is either a sudden reaction to something which has happened to us, or else a preconceived action which we have thought over beforehand. In other words, either we do things in haste, or else we think about them before we take action. Fasting is not something which we should hurry into; it is not a duty which we can decide about after only a moment's hesitation. It is a practice which will demand some forethought; we shall have to consider *what* it entails and, most important of all, we shall need to know *why* we shall do it. There are all sorts of reasons why men have stopped eating food, in the past. Before we consider these reasons, however, and before we ascertain the biblical purpose of fasting, we must face up to the fact that there are a number of objections to this discipline. Some of them may appear frivolous, but they are all valid in the minds of some readers.

1. *It is more important to fast from sin, than from food.* This objection is expected to produce either silence or a denial from people who uphold fasting as a discipline for christians today. Those who raise this point are surprised to discover that the mature contender for correct fasting is in full agreement with the objection! God does require us to fast from sin, as we see clearly in Isaiah 58:1–14, but also—as those verses show—He is more concerned about fasting from sin than from food. If God has chosen any fast at all, it is certain that it is that we should cease sinning; the discipline of heart and mind is the supreme discipline. However, this does not mean that christians should not ever fast in the way described in these pages. All believers should long for inner holiness, and use all the means of grace provided in order to become what God is calling them to be, but this does not suggest an end of personal disciplines.

2. *It is superstitious to say that God demands this burden today.* This objector holds to the view that the Lord has been slowly changing His image and intentions over the centuries; the idea is that He was brutal in Old Testament times, became more loving in New Testament times and is now sentimental. This objection, therefore, is based upon a false understanding of the Almighty and a peculiar interpretation of the Gospel. In any case, none of the Lord's commands is considered to be hard to bear, by the devout believer. Further, the word superstitious—if

27

applied to the teaching of the Word of God—must be regarded as being out of place.

3. *It is not natural to go without food.* If this objector has moved in circles where fasting is unknown, or where there has been no study of natural diet, his is an understandable attitude. However, for those who have watched the behaviour of animals, in all kinds of situations, this objection is nonsensical. If a member of a lower order of life is unwell, it stops eating immediately, or else eats grass only. Even a domestic animal, when sick, will cease eating, despite the pleas of the owner, until it knows that the disorder has been corrected. Nature knows that the body has self-healing properties which can cope with most animal illnesses, if it is left alone. Also, a wild animal does not always eat every day; sometimes it goes for several days without food, after having eaten well; many captive animals are fed only six days a week. It is, therefore, ludicrous to say that fasting is unnatural—especially in view of the proven physiological benefits, in most conditions.

4. *It is a Roman Catholic doctrine.* We have here an objection which arises from both misunderstanding and prejudice. Are all Roman Catholic doctrines false? Can we reject a teaching just because heretics and heathen also embrace it? Is it always correct procedure to oppose everything that is taught by the Roman Catholics, as though some principle of reciprocation is involved? The average Protestant shies away from fasting of the Roman Catholic *variety* because it is improperly practised. It is the method employed, and the teaching that there is *merit* in the discipline, which give offence and create this objection. Any unbiblical behaviour gives offence to the spiritually minded; a correct observance of fasting can give offence only to those who are unspiritual.

5. *Fasting was fitting for the disciples after the Crucifixion, but it is no longer necessary.* This objection arises

from some comments made by a few theologians on the verses Matthew 9:14–15 and Luke 5:33–35, and was considered in the previous chapter. Their theory suggests that there is no need for fasting during the years between the Ascension and the Final Return of Christ, since He is, by virtue of His salvation, within every believer and not far away from them. If this suggestion is correct (and it should be noted that this idea is not upheld by the most reliable of commentators), then the fastings related in the Acts of the Apostles were foolish. If believers accept this theory, in the face of all the other evidence given in the previous chapter, they must concede that it is based upon only *one* quotation from the lips of Jesus, and can be balanced by more than one in the other direction.

6. *It is better to abstain from jealousy and pride than from food.* This objection is not the same as that raised under number one; the two named sins (or another two, as the case may be) are forms of misbehaviour which the objector has selected for a special reason, known only to himself, or the person with whom he disagrees. This objection is only an 'eye for an eye' philosophy raised in the face of a strong case. The objector has no intention of agreeing with the matter in hand, and seeks only to confuse the other party with a red herring of an objection. All sin is wrong, but to do the will of God is always right.

7. *I have tried it a few times and saw no difference in myself or my prayer life.* This objection is sincere and must be considered honestly. Anyone who has dared to obey the teaching of the Bible should be treated graciously. However, it is obvious that the person concerned has not approached the subject in the correct way. One could make the same remark about repentance, receiving communion, and a dozen other things. What difference did the person expect? Had he been told that if he fasted he would become a changed man, see visions, hear the voice of God, and so

on (all of which might have been said to him by an extremist)? If so, then it is not surprising if he is disappointed. If this same person approaches the subject in a scriptural way, he is likely to cease making this objection. Since 'Jesus assumed that His hearers practised fasting',[1] christians should persevere in their application of the discipline until it has meaning and value.

AVERTING GOD'S WRATH

After hearing some word of doom, countless men—and even whole nations—have turned to fasting in the hope that true repentance would save them from the wrath of God. When the children of Israel were faced with impending doom at the hand of the children of Benjamin, they went to Bethel, sat before the Lord, wept 'and fasted that day until evening' (Judges 20:24-28). When the children of Israel realised that they were suffering national disgrace because of their false worship and ungodly behaviour, they 'gathered together at Mizpah, and drew water, and poured it out before the Lord, and fasted on that day, and said, We have sinned against the Lord', at the summons of Samuel (1 Samuel 7:5-6). When Ezra and Nehemiah sought to re-introduce obedient worship, the children of Israel assembled 'with fasting, and with sackcloth . . . and confessed their sins and the iniquities of their fathers' (Nehemiah 9:1-3). When Joel informed the people that destruction was at hand, he advised that they 'sanctify a fast . . . and cry unto the Lord' (Joel 1:13-14), and when Jonah informed the citizens of Nineveh that their city was to be overthrown, the people 'believed God, and they proclaimed a fast' (Jonah 3:1-10). In each of these cases, large numbers of people realised that the wrath of God was shortly to be revealed to them and so they undertook to repent both inwardly and outwardly, spiritually, mentally, and physically; we are glad to note that the expected wrath of God was averted.

Apart from the use of biblical fasting as a means by which large numbers seek the face of God in unison, there are instances of individuals taking this action on behalf of others. For example, Moses fell down before the Lord, neither eating nor drinking, on behalf of the stiff-necked people of Israel (Deuteronomy 9:18); Ezra fasted on behalf of the sinful people of Israel (Ezra 9:3–5 and 10:6); Nehemiah fasted on behalf of the needy remnant for 'certain days' (Nehemiah 1:4); and the Psalmist fasted for his enemies (Psalm 35:13).

If the man of God, who was sent to denounce the false worship at Bethel, in Jeroboam's reign, had not broken the fast which God had appointed, he would have been saved from an unfortunate end, at the hand of God (1 Kings 13:9 and 19). By comparison, when the people took heed of God's call for a sanctified fast, through the ministry of Joel (Joel 2:12–18), the Lord had mercy on them and blessed them. Clearly, it is wise to heed the call of God if we wish to avert His anger. One saint in the early church, Basil (A.D. 326–380), said that the animal world was aware of this, and that this is why the lions did not eat Daniel (Daniel 6:22), and the whale did not digest Jonah (Jonah 2:10)—as the biblical texts appear to suggest!

EMOTION REACTION

Apart from those who do not eat for fear of the consequences, there are those who cannot eat, for reasons connected with human emotions. When the mind and spirit are suffering deeply, the body often reacts violently, and sometimes all thought of food leaves us completely. The Psalmist informs us that as some unbelievers approach death they become so *anxious* at heart, that 'their soul aborreth all manner of meat' (Psalm 107:18); Hannah was unable to eat, as she *ruminated* upon her barren state and the mocking words of her rival (1 Samuel 1:7); Saul was so *distressed* by the news of a possible Philistine victory, that he refused to eat bread 'all the day and all the night' (1 Samuel 28:19–25); 'Jonathan arose from the table in *fierce anger* and did eat no meat' when he heard of his father's attitude towards David (1 Samuel 20:34); Jesus said that He could not eat earthly food, because He had 'meat to eat that you know not of' (John 4:32); Ahab could not eat because of either *covetousness* or *jealousy* when Naboth refused to sell his garden (1 Kings 21:2–6); when the Psalmist was *distressed* he forgot to eat his bread (Psalm 102:4); Elihu told Job that when we are '*chastened* with pain' we are likely to hate food (Job 33:19–20); the soldiers and sailors in charge of the ship taking Paul to Rome were so *worried* about the safety of both the vessel and themselves that they went without food for fourteen days (Acts 27:21 and 33); David was so *sad* at the death of Abner that he could not 'taste bread, or aught else, till the sun be down' (2 Samuel 3:33–36); the psalmist was so *hungry for God* that he wrote 'My tears have been my meat day and night' (Psalm 42:3); King Darius 'passed the night fasting' because of his *misery* about the fate of Daniel, whom he had thrown to the lions (Daniel 6:18); David and his valiant men were so *broken-hearted* at the loss of Saul and Jonathan that they 'mourned, and wept, and fasted until evening' (2 Samuel 1:11–12 and 1 Chronicles 10:12); and Paul was so stricken by the revelation that he had been persecuting the Lord's Christ that he was three days without either food or drink (Acts 9:9).

WATCHINGS AND FAST DAYS

When Paul wrote to the Corinthians about the difficulties of his ministry he said that he had been 'in afflictions, in necessities, in distresses, in stripes, in imprisonments, in tumults, in labour, in watchings, and in fastings' (2 Corinthians 6:4–5). It has been suggested by modern scholars that these experiences were all inflicted upon him, and so the last two named disciplines were actually undertaken involuntarily. However, as Bengel pointed out, these experiences are arranged in three classes; the first three are *general*, the second three are *specific*, and the third *voluntary*. Paul's labours, watchings, and fasts may have been a part of that which he had to suffer for Christ, but he undertook them willingly. This is made quite clear in 2 Corinthians 11:27 where *hunger* and *fasting* are mentioned together in the same sentence. What does it mean to 'watch'?

When Jesus spent long hours in the Garden, just before His Crucifixion, it is said that He was *watching*. Also, when our Lord exhorted people to be ready for His Final Return, He told them to *watch*. In the same vein, Paul included this word, at the end of his advice about the wearing of spiritual armour, saying that christians should *watch* in all perseverance. The word which Paul chose, when he said that he had been in *watchings*, implies that you chase sleep away deliberately, in order to be intent upon something. Sleep is sacrificed so that spiritual truth which cannot otherwise be obtained, may be grasped, and so that spiritual victories may be won. Such *watchings* are often linked to *fasting*. As Bishop Hooper wrote: 'Those who abstain from food in order that the spirit may be more ardent, and the mind given to study and prayer, do well.' 'There is much evidence that Jonathan Edwards was punctual, constant, and frequent in secret prayer, and often kept days of fasting and prayer in secret.'[2]

Jesus did not fast in the wilderness for forty days because it was a regular discipline; he was 'led of the Spirit'[3] to do it. If a christian is abstemious and, therefore, willing to

33

deny himself at any time when the occasion demands it, this call of the Holy Spirit to a season of spiritual refreshment is not uncommon. 'Jesus was well aware that His Father had subjected Him to the discipline of this fast for precisely the same purpose that Israel had been "suffered to hunger" in the wilderness; it was that the supreme lesson might be learned that *man shall not live by bread alone, but by every word that proceedeth out of the mouth of God*. The Father, Who had called Him and submitted Him to temptation, would in His own good time supply the physical necessities of His Son. The duty of Jesus was to be obedient to that call, and not to decide for Himself either the moment or the manner in which His fast should be ended.'[4] Such a duty may be assigned to the followers of Christ, if the Father so chooses, but the duration of the fast is not likely to be forty days.

FAST DAYS

Apart from private and personal days of fasting and prayer, in seasons of watching with Christ, fasting has a purpose in what have been called Fast Days. As far as the christian is concerned, these began in Old Testament times after the ministry of Moses, and soon after the Jews had settled in their own land. The first clear example is given in 1 Samuel 7:5-6, where it is evident that this was an established practice. In general, it can be said that these Fast Days were special, and were proposed by men, not God. The only fast which we are sure was God-appointed was the Day of Atonement discipline mentioned in chapter one. Sometimes the prophets spoke as if God was the author of their ideas but only in the Levitical enunciation is this made perfectly lucid. However, by the time that Christ commenced His ministry, it was perfectly normal for people to call for a day of fasting for some reason or other (Jeremiah 36:9). Esther did not hesitate to institute

34

fasting when she saw the size of the crisis (Esther 4:16), and took the correct action, without doubt. We have every reason, however, to doubt the wisdom of Mordecai in exhorting all Jews to commemorate, on two special days, the victory which the Queen had achieved (Esther 9:21, 27 and 31). Indiscriminate days of fastings like this resulted in there being many established Fast Days in the time of our Lord,[5] and most Pharisees fasted twice a week (Luke 18:11–12).

Since we are living in an age that neglects fasting, it is difficult to remember the last time when there was a call for a Civic, or National, Fast in a western country. It is considered that the last of these in the United Kingdom was requested in 1853 (the year of a bad cholera epidemic). That call, however, was rejected by Lord Palmerston, on the grounds that there was a more obvious urgency for hygiene. A recent, and interesting, Day of Fasting was held on the 5th June 1967, following a call by the Chief Rabbi, on behalf of Israel, regarding the Jewish/Arab war.

Fast Days were, however, quite common in some periods of history. For example, the Diary of Samuel Pepys includes eighteen references to special Days of Fasting, within the space of ten years, including one on Wednesday the 30th January 1661 as a sign of the nation's repentance for the 'murder' of Charles I, the 'late king'. Also, in 1572, Edwin Sandys the Bishop of London (and five years later to become the Archbishop of York) proposed a day of public fasting and prayer 'for the confounding of the cruel enemies of God's Gospel', after news came to England of the appalling massacre of many thousands of Huguenots in Paris, and other large French cities, by the Roman Catholics.

Fast Days appear to have followed the three-fold pattern of being Civic Fasts, appointed by, and subject to, national or local government, Congregational Fasts, appointed by, and subject to, Church leaders, and Personal Fast Days appointed by either oneself or God. That there have been national fasts instituted, for special reasons, by the Lord, is undeniable in the face of such texts as Joel 1:13-14. However, as Henry Barrow wrote, public fasting is—in general—'an action belonging to the church, to be used upon special occasions, as in the time of some public calamity ... That public fasts have always belonged to the church, and been exercised therein, plentifully appeareth in the Old and New Testaments.'[6]

SEEKING GOD'S PARDON

As we have seen, fasting has often been undertaken as a means by which unbelieving men have averted God's wrath. In a similar way, believers have taken to fasting—after having fallen into sin—in order to re-discover God's pardon. Penitence is an essential ingredient of biblical fasting, so it is natural for christians to seek God through self-denial if they become aware of an unsatisfied need for divine pardon. 'If man, in hope of getting pardon, will humble himself to those of whom he has no promise, in order to receive something, how much more ought we to humble ourselves in the presence of the One who has made sure promises.'[7] Ahab's behaviour, when he became aware of his sin, attracted God's pleasure: 'Seest thou how Ahab humblest himself before Me?' (1 Kings 21:27-29). This does not mean that mere fasting from food alone achieves any benefit; the abstinence must be subservient to the inner spiritual exercise. To refrain from food, when one's mind and heart are very much engaged with serious matters of the heart, is a natural bodily expression of one's sense of unworthiness. 'Blessed are they that mourn, for they shall be comforted' (Matthew 5:4).

The fact that 'all eminently pious persons have been more or less addicted'[8] to fasting, proves that it has a personal spiritual value. John the Baptist appears to have practised partial fasting constantly (Matthew 3:4 and 11:18-19, Mark 1:6), Anna 'served God with fastings and prayers, night and day' (Luke 2:36-37), Paul was 'in fastings often' (2 Corinthians 11:27), and Howel Harris lived on bread and water only, at times; he fasted for a day, then for two days, and finally for three days a week, in order to separate himself for God's work. These people, who are representative of very many more, believed that fasting was an aid to mortification, and so they resorted to it.

When Paul exhorted the christians at Rome to make 'no provision for the flesh' (Romans 13:14), the ones at Colosse to 'mortify your members' (Colossians 3:5), informed those at Corinth that he kept his body under, in order to 'bring it into subjection' (1 Corinthians 9:25-27), and assured those in Galatia that christians 'have crucified the flesh with affections' (Galatians 5:24), he was stating the case for Mortification. In the *unbeliever* there is only one abiding principle at work, and this ensures that he is under the dominion of sin. In the *believer* there are two principles at work; he now has the Holy Spirit within him, by whose power he may overcome the other sinful active force. This is not to say that fasting is the *only* aid to mortification; it is only this to the ascetic and the extremist. The christian relies upon the Holy Spirit to enable him to 'mortify' his unruly nature; on occasions, however, he resorts to fasting as one aid to mortification.

This is the main theme of the teaching of Isaiah 58:1-14. The children of Israel had lost all sense of communion with God and their seasonal fasts had become valueless. 'Mere external religion and outward conformity to ritual are easy

37

Moreover they tend to produce a spirit of self-satisfaction. What meets with God's approval is that obedience to His Word, which firstly keeps the soul in true exercise of heart before Him, and then leads to the fulfilment of all righteousness in our ways and relationships with others.'[9] Instead of loosing the 'bonds of wickedness', in their own hearts, and 'breaking every yoke' within them, as they fasted, these Jews were fasting outwardly only. The Levitical fast 'signified the mortifying of sin, and turning from it.'[10] 'Sorrow does not take away the sin, but it takes away the taste for it, and the pleasant taste of it; it does not empty out the vessel, but it frees the emptied vessel (i.e. the pardoned soul) from the former relish it had for earth.'[11]

As John Chrysostom (A.D. 347–407) made abundantly clear, fasting is of no value unless all other proper duties accompany it. For this reason, our Lord did not isolate the discipline, when He commented upon it, but linked it with christian duties towards both God and man: prayer and alms-giving. When fasting takes its proper place in the life of a christian, it is an aid to the mortification of the old man and a stimulant for the envigoration of the new man.

KEEPING THE BALANCE

From this, it will be seen that fasting is one way by which a believer may keep the balance between the things which are spiritual and those which are only physical. 'The outward abstinence, which has the effect of pulling down the body, helps to lift up the mind.'[12] Nobody can maintain a desired state of mind whilst his bodily condition is not in accordance with it. If a man is anxious to devote himself to spiritual things, for a time, he is obliged to ensure that his body is in a similar environment, or else he may not succeed. He cannot be reverent in the midst of his own physical irreverence. Fasting ensures the correct environment for sorrowful and serious considerations. Asterius wrote, in the 4th. Century, that one role of fasting is to ensure that the stomach does not make the body boil like a kettle, to the hindering of the soul.

'Christians are not exempt from the temptation to let the body master them. The tendency is to spend more time in eating than in feeding mind and soul with the Word of God. A simple check on personal daily habits will prove the truth of this. Most of us feel a more pressing need to keep fit physically, than to take spiritual exercise. Both are necessary, but few keep the balance between them. In consequence, many are overweight physically and under-nourished spiritually.'[13]

Dr. John Lightfoot, rector of Great Munden in Hertfordshire, 'preached both morning and evening each Lord's Day. He often continued in the church the whole day and scrupulously abstained from all food until the evening service had been completed, so that he might be more intent upon his sacred duties.'[14]

DESIRE FOR SPECIAL MERCY

Another use to which fasting has been put repeatedly, is connected to the believer's need for special help from God. When David, following his hasty marriage to Bathsheba, became the father of a child which was clearly dying from birth, the first thing that he thought of was his need to seek the Lord for mercy; 'David therefore besought God for the child; he fasted and lay all night upon the earth' (2 Samuel 12:15-23). When Jehoshaphat learned that a great army was on its way to destroy his people, he 'set himself to seek the Lord, and proclaimed a fast throughout all Judah' (2 Chronicles 20:2-3). When Ezra realised his need of protection, for himself and those with him, against his enemies, he 'proclaimed a fast at the river Ahava, so that we might humble ourselves before our God, to seek of Him a straight way' (Ezra 8:21–23). When Esther saw the urgency of the moment, and the plight of the Jews, she called for a three-day fast (Esther 4:1–17).

This does not mean that every christian may be assured of an answer to prayer if he begins to fast as well as beseech God; in the case of David, just related, the prayer for healing of the newly-born child was not answered. Therefore, it is not fasting *alone* which causes God to answer prayer. Nevertheless, God does see fit to bless believers who turn to Him in prayer with fasting, having contrite hearts and humility. Because of this, we read of many occasions down through the centuries when christian people gathered for seasons of prayer and fasting, in order to intreat God for a time of religious revival, and spiritual awakening.

Roman Catholic theologians have commented that Protestants do not fast and so are disobedient to Christ's call. Alert Protestants have replied that this is mere presumption since christian fasting is done in secret, and so the extent of it is not known by any human being, and is incorrect anyway, since Roman Catholic fasting is pharisaical fasting, and is itself contrary to the teaching of the Bible on the subject. In general, Protestants have been shy about fasting because they have used it mostly in the realm of personal worship and communion with Christ. In the sixteenth century, however, congregational fasts were quite common and attracted people from places many miles distant.

'The Exercise consisted of a "humbling and casting down" and a "profession of our faith, that we shall be lifted up as high, through the grace of the Lord our God in Jesus Christ, as the conscience of our sins doth cast us down". In other words, the fast was an occasion for instruction in the protestant doctrine of repentance, and this was to be "fetched from the public preaching of the Word". It was to last for at least a whole day. "And if the wrath of the Lord be hotter, then two days or else three." It could be private, of a particular man, or household.'[15]

To fast in order to appear to be devout is hypocritical, as we shall see in the chapter on *Dangers*, but to deny oneself food in order to encourage a private sense of awe is helpful—as long as it is only resorted to on rare occasions. In this sense, fasting is a holy exercise, since it stirs up the right kind of thinking towards God and humbles the person concerned.

In Nehemiah 9:3, we read that the children of Israel, on one occasion, divided their fast into four parts, of which the last part took the form of *worship*. In Luke 2:36–37, we read that Anna linked her fasts with *service for God, in prayers*. In Acts 13:2, we read that Barnabas and his friends *ministered unto the Lord* as they fasted. In Acts 14:23 we note that Paul and his colleagues had a time of worship with fasting *after* they had ordained some of the men as elders. And in Daniel 9:3, we read that Daniel sought the face of God by 'prayer and supplications, with fasting'. Clearly, the people of God have made a habit of linking fasting with intimate worship, from the beginning.

Charles Haddon Spurgeon related that 'our seasons of fasting and prayer at the Tabernacle have been high days indeed; never has Heaven's gate stood wider; never have our hearts been nearer the central Glory.'[16] Paget Wilkes recorded that at one of the annual conventions of the Japanese Evangelistic Band, the 'dear saints met together for fasting and intercessory prayer. There was no address and very little singing, but a continual stream of prayer for

41

Japan in all its counties. One C.M.S. worker said that it was the most wonderful prayer meeting she had ever attended.'[17]

THE PURPOSE OF FASTING

It may be said, therefore, that fasting has many purposes, or else that its purpose has many facets. There are private fasts, partial fasts, special fasts, extreme fasts, civic fasts, congregational fasts, involuntary fasts, and fastings unawares—the observance of which may be quite scriptural; however, not all of these are promised a reward.

'It was not merely by the light of reason, or of natural conscience—as it is called—that the people of God have been, in all ages, directed to use fasting as a means; but they have been, from time to time, taught it of God Himself, by clear and open revelations of His Will. Now, whatever reasons there were to quicken those of old, in the zealous and constant discharge of this duty, they are of equal force still to quicken us.'[18]

NOTES

[1] Arthur S. Peake in his 'Commentary on the Bible' p. 706
[2] From an account of Edward's life by Serono Dweight which is related in *Select Works of Jonathan Edwards*: vol. 1, p. 28
[3] Matthew 4:1, Mark 1:12, and Luke 4:1
[4] R. V. G. Tasker: *Commentary on Matthew:* p. 53
[5] Matthew 9:14, Mark 2:18, and Luke 5:33
[6] From Barrow's *A Brief Discoverie of the False Church*: p. 86
[7] From Cartwright's *The Holy Exercise of a True Fast*
[8] Charles Hodge: *Princeton Sermons:* p. 263
[9] W. E. Vine on this passage: *Isaiah:* p. 189
[10] Part of Matthew Henry's comment on Leviticus 16:29–31
[11] Part of Andrew Bonar's comments on Leviticus 23:27–32
[12] From Cartwright's *The Holy Exercise of a True Fast*
[13] John Savage, in an article on Fasting: *Life of Faith:* 9–3–1967
[14] William Urwick: *Nonconformity in Hertfordshire:* p. 596
[15] Patrick Collinson: *The Elizabethaan Puritan Movement:* p. 214
[16] Quoted by E. M. Bounds: *Power through Prayer:* p. 31
[17] M. W. D. Pattison: *The Life Story of Paget Wilkes:* p. 116
[18] John Wesley: *Sermon on Fasting:* 22–2–11

III: The Benefits

'...thy Father shall recompense thee openly...'

When speaking of fasting for the christian, Jesus said that if we did this after the biblical pattern, and in accordance with His advice, and not like the religious hypocrites, we should *receive* something. This reaction to our disciplined action would not be comparable to the reward gained by the Pharisees; they were rewarded by mere men, the humble believer is rewarded by the Father.

The word used by Jesus has special significance for, instead of implying an immediate reward which can be counted in earthly terms, it suggests *restoration* over a period of time. The word He chose to use (as presented in Greek) at the end of verse sixteen, in Matthew chapter six, is different from that used at the end of verse eighteen. The implication is that Phariseeical fasting (praying and giving, also) has an immediate reward in the applause of men, but true christian fasting need not have any apparent benefit straight away. The Father's *recompense* has an eternal value; basically this *recompense* is spiritual, even though it creates physical features also. In other words, the benefits of fasting are 'added extras' which come to christians 'by the way'. If we use fasting in order to obtain some benefit, as though it were a tool in our hands, we may find ourselves in spiritual extremism or suffering frustration. If we fast for the right reasons, we shall notice that we have gained some benefits unawares. 'If we are sincere in our solemn fasts, and humble, and trust God's omniscience for our witness, and His goodness for our recompense, we shall find, both that He did see in secret, and will recompense openly. Religious fasts, if rightly kept, will shortly be recompensed with an everlasting feast.'[1]

43

Therefore, in one sense, it is a huge task to list the benefits of this discipline; as Bishop Jeremy Taylor wrote: 'He who would recount the benfits of fasting, might just as well, in the next page, attempt to enumerate the benefits of medicine.'

It would be easy to gain the impression that many of the fasts recorded in the Old Testament, and some of those mentioned in the New Testament, were undertaken in order to encourage God to give those who fasted what they wanted; a superficial reading of the Bible could lead some to this conclusion. However, we know that God is not inclined to respond to such approaches, despite the teaching of some extremists that almost any divine blessing is available to those who will take up the practice of fasting.[2] Because of the false notions which have circulated about this discipline, it will be wise if we preface our thoughts about *benefits* by a consideration of the *grounds* upon which a believer may fast.

Any blessing which is bestowed by the Father upon his undeserving children, must be considered to be an act of grace. We fail to appreciate the mercy of the Lord if we think that by our *doing something* we have forced (or even coerced) God to grant that blessing which we have asked for. If one can understand the words of our Lord in Matthew 6:8, He always knows in advance what we are going to pray about. Indeed, if our prayers are in accordance with the mind of Christ, harmonise with the will of God, and are energised by the Holy Spirit, our words will voice requests which He has put into our hearts Himself; we shall be requesting *His* desires. Christian prayer is not man *pre*scribing to God, but *sub*scribing. All of our fasting, therefore, must be on this basis; we should use it as a scriptural means whereby we are melted into a more complete realisation of the purposes of the Lord in our life, church, community, and nation.

'Christians who abstain from food and from the gratifying of other normal appetites, in order to give themselves to prayer with undivided attention, have testified to the liberty of spirit which they have enjoyed and to the depth and height of their communion with God at such times.'[3]

'How shall we obtain ability to pray with fervour in times of need, if first the coals of the Spirit are not kindled within us by the bellows of God's Word—the preaching of which is not so fruitful as it would be, without both public and private prayer, nor prayer so fervent as it should be without fasting. The want of one results in preaching without fruit, the ignorance of the other has starved our prayers of feeling, the lack of both (which should have gone together) has frozen us.'[4] When the body is not replete with food, the mind can work more efficiently, and the spirit is liberated.

If we are to have any object in view, when we set out to abstain from food for religious reasons, the first one ought to be that we desire a deeper communion with Christ. If fasting has this basis, it may be anticipated that there will be liberty in prayer.

RECEIVING GUIDANCE

Most christians believe in guidance, and although some *have* gone astray, piling their lives upon the rocks, through unscriptural methods, God *does* still guide and lead His people. What do you do if the way ahead is not clear? Guidance is not always obtained by the kind of automatic response facilities which some have claimed. There are times when our Lord does not wish to give us explicit details very far ahead; on such occasions silence is the answer to our pleas. The subject of guidance cannot be reduced to a few sentences here, and so other books should be consulted for more light on this matter.[5]

However, we can see that the Apostles were used to the idea of fasting, when in need of divine aid. 'Now there were at Antioch, in the Church that was there, prophets and teachers ... and as they ministered to the Lord, and *fasted*, the Holy Ghost said "Separate me Barnabas and Saul for the work whereunto I have called them". Then, when they had *fasted* and prayed and laid their hands on them, they sent them away. So, they, being sent forth by the Holy Ghost, went down to Seleucia' (Acts 13:1-3). We are given the impression that the experience of fasting provided such a vital fellowship with the Holy Spirit, that a better environment for guidance was created. This is not to say that fasting is a *guarantee* for guidance; the point is that those who fast are placing themselves in a situation through which the Holy Spirit has an easier access to them. On Monday, the 19th April 1742, David Brainerd 'set apart this day for fasting and prayer to God for His grace, especially to prepare me for the work of the ministry: *to give me divine aid and direction* in my preparations for that great work, and in his own time to send me into His harvest.'[6]

GROWTH IN GRACE

When God first gave instructions concerning the religious discipline of fasting, He said that His people were to 'afflict their souls'. As we have seen in the first chapter, if we afflict our souls we *humble ourselves*; the original basic reason for fasting was the human need for abasement. It follows from this that those who fast, in this biblical (and correct) way, become humble. By this we must not conclude that the act of fasting has some virtuous power, and that *we* have made ourselves more humble; there is no

46

virtue in fallen man by which he can make himself more godly; there is, however, virtue in the divinely appointed means of grace. If we, by the power of the Holy Spirit, mortify the deeds of the body, we shall grow in grace, but the glory of such change will be God's alone.

When the early people of God fasted, they clothed themselves in sackcloth (1 Kings 20:31, Nehemiah 9:1, Esther 4:1–4, Psalm 35:13 and 69:11, Daniel 9:3, Joel 1:13, and Jonah 3:5), and even took off their ornaments (e.g. Exodus 33:5), in order to do all *in their power* to humble themselves before their sovereign Lord. Whilst it must be admitted that there were many who acted the part, but were not affected inwardly (as Isaiah 58:1–14 suggests), this experience was a source of spiritual benefit to a few, at least. Further, this annual season of personal, and national, abasement gave God's people deep insight concerning the sovereignty of God and their own complete reliance upon Him; this is the basis for growth in grace.

INCREASES IN FAITH

So many christians bemoan their lack of faith, not realising that it is often their own fault that they are faithless. We are told that each christian is given a measure of faith[7] and so it is obvious that we must have failed to use that which was given, if we do not appear to have it now. Fasting does not *create* faith, for faith grows in us as we hear, read, and dwell upon, God's Word; it is a work of the Holy Spirit to bring faith to God's people. However, fasting has the capacity to *encourage* faith in the one who is involved in this discipline. It seems as though the neglect of self feeds the faith which God has implanted in the hearts of born-again believers. This does not mean that those who eat the least have the most faith; such a view is not only untrue, it is extremist. It is simply that regular

47

self-denial has its benefits, and one of these is seen in a personal increase in faith. As J. A. Alexander has pointed out,[8] if even Apostles rely upon their extraordinary powers alone, and forget the spiritual discipline which is essential to the pastoral office, they will be ineffective through a deficiency of faith, in a crisis. Or, as John Wesley put it, prayer and fasting 'are the appointed means' by which unusual faith is attained.[9]

POWER OVER EVIL

From thoughts of the benefit of *having* an increase in faith, it is natural for us to think to what *purpose* this increase might be put, in view of the despairing cry of the Apostles 'Why could not we cast it out?' (Matthew 17:19, Mark 9:28, and Luke 9:40). If we have ever sat down and enjoyed a continuous perusal of the Gospel of Luke, we will know of the exhilaration that can be imparted from the fourth chapter. In the fourteenth verse we read that Jesus returned to Galilee from the wilderness 'in the power of the Spirit'. Our Lord had just completed a remarkable fast in complete isolation, and had suffered intense temptations at the close of the same. The picture which Luke painted, is of One Who had complete mastery over all evil. To have been with Jesus at that point in His life would have been most memorable.

However, one gains the impression that our Lord considered it possible that His disciples might have similar power over evil, from such verses as Matthew 10:1, Luke 9:1 and 10:19. Can christians have power over 'all of the enemy'? They cannot have such power, we must acknowledge, unless the Lord gives it to them, in the same way that he *gave* authority to His first disciples. Power with God cannot be won or earned—it can only be received. If, however, this power is received by a believer, he will need to spend much time—day by day—in prayer, and he must resort to fasting often. An undisciplined christian cannot keep precious divine gifts; the treasure leaks away. Those who seem to have a superabundance of faith, in the face of evil, are those who are much in prayer.

It is no use asking advice about this from those who have not fasted at any time and who deride this discipline now. If we want proof of the connection between self-denial and spiritual power, we must go to those who have moved many with their words and helped large numbers to find faith in Jesus Christ. Those who are most mighty with God are those who confess openly that they are a failure unless the Holy Spirit is upon them. Luther wrote 'He who is poor has nothing to fear: he has nothing to lose. I have no property, and desire none. If I possessed any prestige and honour—well, he who loses them now will simply continue to lose them. There is only one thing left: my poor worn body.'[10]

'Florence Hoskin was made a cripple by the ill-usage of one of her family and wholly lost the use of one of her legs. She had been this way for seven years and was obliged to go on a crutch and a stick. She was so weak that she was forced to drag her foot after her, and her doctor told her that she would not have the use of her leg any more. In 1844, on a Saturday night, she prayed: "Now, my dear Lord, Thou hast healed my soul, why not heal my body, too?" The Lord said to her: "Arise and go down to the Gospel House and there thou shalt be healed". She rose out of her bed to go to the Gospel House to get healed, strong in faith, but when she got downstairs, it was as if the devil stood in the doorway to tempt her to have her breakfast first. She said: "No, devil, I will not, for thou hast many times tempted me to stay for breakfast and I have had a dead meeting through it"... When that meeting was over, she could walk about the chapel without crutch or stick, and came home healed.'[11]

Paul testified that his ministry was in the power and demonstration of the Holy Spirit.[12] Whilst it is true that remarkable spiritual powers in preaching are a definite *gift* of the sovereign will of God, it has been found necessary to *foster* these gifts by acts of self-denial. Fasting is a vital practice for those who are called to preach in an effective way. 'All eminently pious persons have been more or less addicted to this mode of spiritual culture.'[13]

Girolamo Savonarola was a priest in the Dominican Order when he was appointed to the office of Prior of Florence, in 1491. His preaching had always been highly regarded, but now he became a man aflame with truth 'He fasted and prayed; at last he found his message. The sentences rushed out, never halting, never losing intensity or volume, but growing until his voice became as the voice of God Himself. Tears gushed from the eyes of the hearers, they beat their breasts, they cried unto God for mercy, the church echoed with their sobs. These sermons caused such terror, alarm, such tears, that everyone passed through the streets without speaking, more dead than alive.'[14] Often, Savonarola was so weak with fasting, before such preaching, that he needed help to remain in the pulpit.

Charles G. Finney appears to have been empowered immediately after his conversion and always spoke with unction and conviction. 'Sometimes,' he wrote, 'I would find myself, in a great measure, empty of this power. I would then set apart a day for private fasting and prayer, fearing that this power had departed from me. After humbling myself, and crying out for help, the power would return upon me with all its freshness.'[15]

John wrote how he wished that the recipient of his third letter might 'prosper and be in health' even as his soul prospered.[16] He was not enunciating a divine law, since many famous saints have known severe sickness; John was simply praying for a sick friend. However, many of those who have practised fasting have discovered that there is often an improvement in health following physical self-denial of this kind. Fasting, as a means of restoring health, has been employed by physicians for centuries, and so it will not surprise the reader to learn that some practitioners have developed a system of health by an almost exclusive use of fasting. In fact, some authors of books dealing with natural methods of curing oneself, have carried their conclusions to extremes. For example, although it may be of interest to some people that those who undertake long fasts have been known to regain a fine head of hair, this is of no interest to the christian. It must be understood, therefore, that although it is right to include a section on physical well-being, under the heading of *benefits*, this is in no way connected with any selfish urge to recapture youth, or with that common idea which suggests our health is the most important blessing.

We have seen already, that the real benefit of fasting is not in a direct result, but in an indirect blessing. For christians to adopt the attitude that they are going to fast until they get what they want, even though the things that they desire may be ethically acceptable, is dangerous. At least one minister has made it known in his church that he was in the process of fasting until the Lord sent a revival to his congregation, and has been committed to a mental hospital soon afterwards. To use fasting as a lever in one's approach to God is more likely to do harm to the mind than affect the issue. To enter into a long fast, without being instructed

51

to do so from Heaven—only in order to get well—may be good advice from the Nature Cure doctor to the non-christian patient, but could prove harmful to the believer, if he thought that this was essentially religious.

When a christian falls sick, he is wise if he *first* prays and *secondly* seeks a medical opinion; this seems to be the scriptural pattern.[17] For him to presume that he has no need to pray or seek advice, but only to *fast*, does not add up to anyone other than himself.[18] This does not mean that fasting in order to regain health is always wrong; we are at pains only to ensure that one is fully aware of the need to approach the subject with the right motives.

Many christians do not realise the need to eat carefully and temperately, and so sometimes fall foul of disease through ignorance. Dr. H. A. Morton Whitby, a well known surgeon, has shown[19] that over-eating can be as much a sin as the breaking of a commandment, if we believe that our bodies are the temple of the Holy Spirit.[20] He has also shown that fasting can be a genuine source of benefit to christians, from a point of view of general health.[21] Dr. Otto H. F. Buchinger has also made this clear in his book[22] which has a similar approach to the subject. Fasting, therefore, can be a useful means by which christians can balance their manner of living as well as enhance their souls.

More than one believer has become so penitent, over a secret sin, that food could not be eaten for several days, and drink be taken only after insistent pleas; in many of these cases, the general health improved remarkably as well as the inner spiritual life. In some cases, the persons concerned were so pleased at their physical improvement that they began to have a regular weekly day of private fasting in order to keep alert and fit. John Chrysostom wrote in his 'Homilies', in the fourth century, that 'fasting is a medicine'. However, considering that there is no biblical teaching about fasting as a means towards good health, and indeed, no christian doctrine that good health is something to crave for, this whole subject should be kept in correct perspective. If christians fasted regularly they would see the physical improvement quite quickly, and would realise that their well-being is affected by the ancient religious discipline.

POWER OVER CARNALITY

After a certain period of time, many christians realise that their witness is not effective and that their personal life lacks holiness. The joy which once filled them has waned, only to be replaced by a despondency caused through failure. This may well be due to the fact that true conversion has not taken place at all; it is possible for someone to want to become a christian, and make all the mechanical moves towards this end, without being 'born-again', through the operation of the Holy Spirit, in the individual life. On the other hand, a genuine believer can know times of deep despair and inward failure; christian conversion does not hold out a promise of instant sinlessness, or constant overflowing hopefulness.

However, God has provided a dynamic for every believer through His Gospel, and divine energy is still available today; we can share in the fulness of the Holy Spirit. Nevertheless, such an experience is valueless without discipline; there are many saints who face carnality. To maintain power over the desires of the flesh, and to be in constant victory over the egoistic self, we need much of the grace of God. To receive that grace in times of violent temptation, and to enjoy God's power when needed, there is no doubt that we shall find fasting necessary, sometimes. Fasting starves the flesh, allowing the mind to turn towards spiritual issues. If a man, when trying to pray, is constantly faced by pictures which make prayer a mockery, let that man fast—he will begin to taste the presence of God instead.

In the Book of Common Prayer, and in the Collect for the first Sunday in Lent, fasting is defined as 'such abstinence that our flesh may be subdued to the spirit'. Also, we read that 'fasting is designed to strengthen the spiritual life by weakening the attractions of sensible pleasure'.[23] And, fasting 'is a means to curb the flesh and the desires of it, and to make us more lively in religious exercises, as fullness of bread is apt to make us drowsy'.[24]

'Every athlete who goes into training conducts himself temperately and restricts himself in all things. They do it to win a wreath that will soon wither, but we do it to receive a crown of eternal blessedness that cannot wither. Therefore, I do not run uncertainly—without definite aim; I do not box as one beating the air and striking without an adversary. But I *buffet my body—handle it roughly, discipline it by hardships—and subdue it*, for fear that after proclaiming to the others the Gospel and things pertaining to it, I myself should become unfit and rejected as counterfeit.'[25]

It cannot be said that every christian will be saved from all carnality if he takes up fasting. It can be said, however, that fasting is a most powerful aid to those who face this problem. However, in view of the fact that fasting is not mentioned in the list of *means* at the end of Paul's Epistle to the Ephesians, we should be wrong if we elevated this discipline above its proper value.

COPING WITH CRISES

If a crisis appears in our homes we act immediately; this is the natural and obvious thing to do, because a fire demands the use of water, a baby's scream needs attention, and broken glass requires sweeping up. We all understand

54

these things; and even the young, or simple minded, can see danger in such situations. A similar wisdom is made manifest in those who are spiritual, during *spiritual* crises. If a crisis develops in a church through division, heresy, or open sin, a call should be made—by those in authority —for a time of special prayer. If visits from the church, to those who have disgraced it, are of no avail, then it must be presumed that we are face to face with a crisis. The Bible suggests that such a crisis demands action; the prophet of old knew the kind of action that was necessary when he proclaimed 'Call a solemn assembly: sanctify a fast'.[26]

This does not mean that every crisis requires united fasting prayer; only some crises demand this kind of action. However, it can be said that those christians who now fast (in the way outlined in the first and sixth chapters), find themselves more capable of coping with crises than they used to be. Further, having realised the personal value of fasting, they find its use—in a crisis—most rewarding.

When the Presbyterian missionary to Koreans, Bruce F. Hunt heard, in his prison cell, late in 1941, that a mature Korean christian by the name of Choi Han Gee had become mentally deranged, as a result of solitary confinement, he was glad to have an opportunity of meeting him and praying with him. Mr. Hunt was horrified to see the change in someone who had been one of the most consecrated of the local believers; he had turned into a pitiful and unattractive creature. Despite the shortage of food and regardless of the fact that weakness provided easy access to disease, the missionary decided that he must turn to fasting and prayer in order to help Choi. Within a remarkably short time, the weak and emaciated intellectual Korean was not only out of prison, but was of a sound mind. The last that was heard of him, from North Korea, spoke only of his zeal for God in his preaching missions.[27]

NOTES

1 From Matthew Henry's comments on Matthew 6:18

2 Gordon Cove came close to this view in his book *Revival Now through Prayer and Fasting*: Nelson: 1957

3 J. Clement Connell, in an article on Fasting in *The Christian*; 13–3–1964

4 William Wilkinson, in his Preface to the 1580 edition of Cartwright's *The Holy Exercise of a True Fast*

5 For example: *Guidance* by Oliver R. Barclay: I. V. F.: 1956, and *Discovering God's Will* by Yvonne Simms: Hodder: 1965

6 Jonathan Edwards: *The Life of David Brainerd:* p. 26

7 Romans 12:3—This is not initial faith, it is faith for service.

8 See his *Commentary on Mark*: p. 254

9 From Wesley's *Sermon on Fasting*: 22–2–10

10 From Martin Luther's letter to John von Staupitz, dated 30th May 1518

11 F. W. Bourne: *Billy Bray:* pp. 67–9

12 1 Corinthians 2:4

13 Charles Hodge: *Princeton Sermons:* p. 263

14 James Burns: *Revivals—Their Laws and Leaders:* pp. 116–20

15 From the *Lectures on Revivals*, given by Charles G. Finney

16 3 John 2

17 This advice is amplified in the author's two titles *Sickness in Christians* and *Divine Healing*

18 It is possible to gain this notion through reading a lot of non-christian Nature-Cure books which stress abstinence from food, regardless of religion

19 In his book *Preservation of Health*

20 1 Corinthians 6:19

21 In chapter twelve of *Preservation of Health*

22 *About Fasting*

23 *Oxford Dictionary of the Christian Church: p. 495*

24 Part of Matthew Henry's comments on Matthew 6:16

25 Paul in 1 Corinthians 9:25–27, and as translated in the *Amplified Bible*

26 Joel 2:15

27 This story will be found in *For a Testimony* by Bruce F. Hunt, p. 64 ff.

IV: The Dangers

'. . . not like the hypocrites . . .'

We have seen that fasting serves more than one obvious purpose, and also that religious people have taken up the discipline of fasting for more than one reason. Where God has seen fit to commend the person (or persons) concerned, or where fasting prayer has been answered quickly, we may assume that the behaviour has not been wrong, in the eyes of God. Clearly, there are many biblical instances where fasting was desirable, commendable, and wholly godly. However, there are enough cases, on biblical record, in which fasting has been displeasing to God, that we shall do well to note them. For the Lord to declare that someone's fast was 'for strife and contention' (Isaiah 58:4) may appear unbelievable to those who are neither acquainted with the discipline itself, nor the excesses of some religious people. We shall see that this kind of language is not altogether unreasonable, if we consider now the traps into which one may fall.

RITUALISM

It is very easy for a custom, which at some time has been a help to a group of people, to become a ritual. In other words, that which was fresh and inspired one day may, if continued, become a lifeless habit. If fasting becomes a ritual, not only do we lose the point of it, but also we have no benefit from it. 'During the Babylonian exile, as a result of the lack of the sacrificial services, the opinion arose more and more that fasting was a meritorious work, that would be rewarded by God. Thus the practice of fasting assumed an increasingly outward and formal character and lost much of its religious value. For this reason the prophets, during and after the exile, took drastic action against it. True fasting, they proclaimed, consisted not in abstaining from food and drink, but in renouncing sin.'[1] What was true of those Old Testament times became true also of the Church, quite soon after its initiation.

We are told in Matthew 9:14, Mark 2:18–20, Luke 5:33 and 18:12, that the Pharisees fasted either *often*, or *twice a week*. Furthermore, the disciples of John seem to have adopted a similar practice, and were held in high honour because of it. What is more, some of the early christians were so unclear about the relationship between personal discipline and God's grace that *they* instituted a twice-a-week programme of fasts for believers, which did not clash with the phariseeical diary! The human love of order and ritual was permitted to gain the upper hand, and soon the impression was given that fasting was obligatory for christians.

By the second century A.D., and through the dark middle centuries, there was a strong reliance upon ritualism. People fasted because they thought it was the 'done thing', because it was a rule in the Church, or because they thought that if they *didn't* fast they would be looked upon as being irreligious. It was during this period in the life of the Church (almost exclusively Roman Catholic) that it became normal for people to eat fish on Fridays. Whereas the early Church came to the decision that it was good for believers to eat *no food* until three o'clock in the afternoon (15.00 hrs.) on both Wednesdays and Fridays, the practice developed into an eating of no *meat* on those days. In due course, the discipline was reduced to merely 'fish on Fridays'. So common had this practice become by the time of Martin Luther that he, though no stranger to this form of self-denial, was forced to preach against the misuse of it. In modern Catholic theological books for the layman, the subject of biblical fasting is ignored altogether, except in connection with preparation for the Catholic Mass,[2] despite the official declaration of canon 1254 of the Code of Canon Law.

Ritualism really engulfed fasting in the sixth century, when fasting was made obligatory by the Second Council of Orleans. All the confusion about fasting being commanded of God stems from the Didache[3] and this Council. It took the Church one thousand years to see the matter clearly, and even then some godly men were unable to free themselves from the cobwebs of the doctrines that had held sway for so long. When John Wesley outlined the right use of fasting, he mistakenly advised that christians should fast (in a biblical manner, however) on the two weekly days mentioned in the Didache.

As Henry Barrow wrote (in 1590): 'The practice and use of fasting in the Church of Christ, under the Gospel, show that there can be no permanent laws for it, relating to the times and the days. Neither the magistrate, nor the whole Church may set positive laws for public fasts, to be held upon such a day, or in such a month, since they are to be used only upon urgent and special occasions. As for private fasts, there can—much less—be any positive laws made.'[4]

ASCETICISM

Although the Bible abounds in teaching concerning selflessness and self-denial, and although our Lord called those who were following Him to deny themselves and take up their crosses (Mark 8:34), this is far removed from religion through discipline alone. In centuries when the experimental aspect of true religion has been hidden, there has been a revival of the ideas of the Stoics, who considered that they could combat personal vice and impurity through a system of disciplines. Other religions have made a habit of turning to the same theory, knowing nothing of the sanctifying power of the Holy Spirit.

Jerome, that remarkable scholar of the fourth century, became an ascetic in his middle years, as a reaction to the worldliness of the Roman Catholicism of his day. To show how even a learned and saintly man may be misled, let us take note of these words of his: 'My face was pale with fasting, and my mind was raging with desires in a body that was cold. And so, bereft of all help, I lay at the feet of Jesus, I washed them with my tears, I wiped them with my hair, and I subjgated the rebellious flesh with fasting.' Jerome's whole understanding of mortification was undermined by his adoption of asceticism. 'Paul was no ascetic, and certainly did not deny himself food to the extent of making that denial an act of heroism.'[5]

FALSE FASTS

Whilst it may be said truthfully that formal fasting and ascetic fasting are themselves false, there are several forms of fasting (which are not uncommon today) that should be labelled separately since they are quite irreligious and altogether false.

The first of these is, in reality, 'a hunger strike'. This practice is adopted by people who wish to attract attention to some good cause, or else their own plight. Young people have been known to commence a hunger strike in a public place in order to shock passers-by sufficiently to encourage their aid in some charitable concern, or national injustice. To call this *fasting*, in view of the word's religious connotations, is ludicrous, and is obviously a mild attempt to suggest that there is some religious point to the activity. To use fasting as a means of attracting attention for either a personal or social matter defeats the teaching of Jesus relating to the all-important secrecy of true fasting. A hunger strike is neither stoicism nor christianity; in fact, it is exhibitionism, and was unknown in this form in Bible times.

Another *false fast* is what might be termed 'self-starvation'. Those who take up this practice have various strange motives, although they do not realise it. Some wish to be slim, despite their present thin state; others desire to cut personal expenditure to the minimum, for no obvious reason; yet others have an idea that food is sinful. These people have not thought out the reason for their behaviour in a rational way; they have a psychological phobia and are in need of skilful help. Their fasting is the result of a medically known condition, which is not at all religious.

Another, not so common, *false fast* is the 'hunger pact' in which two, or more, people vow never to eat again until the plan they have formulated is fulfilled. There is a perfect biblical illustration of a hunger pact in Acts 23:12 and 21, where we read of a band of Jews plotting to assassinate Paul.

HYPOCRISY

If eccentric fasting appears to be a dangerous form of discipline, let it be said now that hypocrisy is the most subtle of dangers that we shall encounter in fasting. For the Pharisee to say 'I fast twice in the week' (Luke 18:12) was proof of his lack of humility. If we fast in such a way that others are informed publicly of our so-called discipline, we are doing nothing more useful than proving that we are hypocrites at heart. Jesus was never more vehement than when He denounced the people who behaved as though they were religious, when—in actual fact—they were not. Hypocrisy is *pretence*, and pretence has no place in christianity. 'In his first lesson on this subject, Christ showed how it could be used merely to exalt the pride of men; He called attention to the Pharisees (who put on a special appearance when fasting) and warned against this.'[6] He said 'When you fast be not as the hypocrites, of a sad countenance; for they disfigure their faces, that they may appear unto men to fast; verily, I say unto you, they have their reward.' (Matthew 6:16) 'The word translated *have* is used in Hellenistic Greek in receipting bills, and indicates that earthly payment has been made *in full*. All such ostentation reflects an entire disregard of the truth that God sees not as man sees.'[7] 'To seek effect, applause, credit, or gain, by a show of godliness, must be shunned by members of the New Kingdom. It would be better to let men think evil of them, than be tempted to use religion for ulterior ends.'[8]

From Matthew 9:14, we know that people were aware how often the Pharisees fasted, which is ample proof of their hypocrisy. However, these religionists were not the first to fall into the subtle trap of hypocrisy. It might be said that Jezebel stooped even lower than the Pharisees by ordering a season of fasting just prior to the stoning of Naboth (1 Kings 21:9–14). 'It is sad that men, who have—in some measure—mastered their pleasure of sensual wickedness, should be ruined by their pride, which is *spiritual* wickedness, and no less dangerous.'[9] What may be assumed readily is that God knows our hearts and so is never misled, as Jeremiah 14:10–12 makes abundantly clear.

However, it can be said—in faint support of the Pharisees—that at least when they fasted, they did *cease eating*; their fasts may have been ostentatious, but they were days of personal discipline. One cannot say this of the majority of fasts which took place between A.D. 300 and 1500. In the fourth century, Ephraem Syrus wrote that many monks were eating in secret when they were supposed to be fasting, and in the sixteenth century Martin Luther gave vivid descriptions of the huge *feasts* that monks had on fast days, adding 'this kind of fasting has turned out to be a great deal worse than the fasting of the Pharisees'.[10]

One may ask why God instituted a day of fasting if He

foreknew that men would prostitute it in the way that was common during the life of Jesus. The answer is that God only instituted the one fast, and this was enunciated in such a way that it could not lead to hypocrisy, if undertaken in the manner prescribed. The Day of Atonement fast cannot breed conceit if the whole nation (or race) is involved. Hypocrisy can only creep in if men add extra fasts which only *some* undertake. The Pharisees had bound heavy burdens on the shoulders of the Jews which God had no part in; for this reason the Pharisees were condemned by our Lord, and His disciples were warned not to copy them.[11]

If a christian lives in a hostel, or college, with a large number of other people, he will not find it easy to hide the fact that he is missing a meal except when he is away from that environment. If there is only one christian in a home which breeds antagonism towards anything spiritual, a similar problem will occur. In such circumstances the one who is fasting must behave in a perfectly natural way and seek to be indifferent about the opinions of others on this matter. If there is any sign of boasting, or even a mild assertion that this is *right* and *superior*, hypocrisy will gain a foothold quickly.

SELFISHNESS

When we pray, and when we offer worship, we ought to be aware of the will of God and be willing for that will to be revealed to us. If our worship is deliberately out of harmony with God's will, or if we are careless as to what God's will is, then our worship is basically selfish; fasting can be an act of selfishness.

We do well if we remember David, that great leader who committed adultery with a beautiful girl called Bathsheba, and then contrived the death of Bathsheba's husband Uriah. He arranged for Bathsheba's husband to die so that he could marry the girl whom he desired, and by whom he was an expectant father. When a child was born as a result of this union it quickly became ill, and looked as if it would die. David, overcome with remorse, fasted and prayed for a week. He seems to have thought that if prayer would bring deliverance, his union with Bathsheba was acceptable to God. The people of those days connected all disease with sin and so, therefore, if the child died everyone would say that the Lord was angry with David.

David fasted and prayed for one week, despite the fact that God had told him of the death beforehand. His motive was purely selfish in seeking to force providence to make things look right for him; there was no answer from Heaven; his fasting came to nothing (2 Samuel 12:15–23).

This frank biblical story may be compared with that told of Pastor Hsi in one of the China Inland Mission's books: 'Two Chinese preachers, who had quarrelled seriously, came to Pastor Hsi about their difference, each accusing the other and demanding his dismissal. Receiving them hospitably into his home, Hsi retired to his room, remaining there for two days without food . . . At the end of two days the Lord gave him the inward assurance that the victory was won, and he came out to see the men. After a few words about the necessity for the confession of personal sin, and the futility of throwing the blame on to others, he started to tell them that the Lord had convicted him of the mistake he had made in ever putting the two of them to work together. He saw now that they were temperamentally unsuited, and that he should have prayed more about the matter before appointing their work. The two men were completely melted, each confessing his own unchristian attitude and behaviour, and with the tears rolling down their cheeks, all three of them knelt together, and were filled anew with the Holy Spirit.'[12]

When George Whitefield visited Scotland in 1742, he

was urged not to preach in the national kirks by those who had seceded from the Church of Scotland. Whitefield ignored these requests, although he understood them, and continued to preach where he was welcomed. At Cambuslang there was an outstanding revival of religion, resulting in the conversion of very many people. The seceders, assured that no good could come from the preaching of one who had spurned their pleas, announced a day of fasting 'for the delusion at Cambuslang'. Whitefield asked for an interview with those who had pressed for this fast to be announced, and quite overwhelmed them by his charitable affection, obtaining a complete apology for the 'hot-blooded' action.[13]

Selfish fasts were denounced by the Lord in Zechariah 7:1–7, when He said 'Did you at all fast unto Me, even to Me?' and in Matthew 6:16–18, when He said 'They have their reward'.

EXTREMISM

There is always somebody who will take any subject to ridiculous lengths, and begin to make claims which are neither reasonable nor practicable. Fasting is not an exception to the general rule and so has been the cause of more than one brand of extremism. Fanaticism has not yet ceased to raise its head in our midst and so we may benefit from a consideration of its effects upon the subject before us.

In the early seventies of the sixteenth century, the puritan practice of holding 'holie exercises' began to develop into a social fashion. Days of fasting and prophesying began to attract all and sundry, and were no longer as serious (and certainly not as sanctifying) as they had been. By 1581, this extremist fasting movement was in full flood and had all the signs of causing lasting harm to the churches in England. Although Eusebius Paget had defined a fast as being a possible action 'by which the faithful prepare themselves to prayer when they take in hand some earnest matter', and although Thomas Cartwright had insisted that it was not to be practised without an obvious good reason, it did become a bandying point for those who had political ambition, and a source of strife for those who wished to 'lord it' over the rest. It is no wonder that the non-christian onlookers scoffed at this unseemly attitude towards public self-denial and coined the phrase 'gadding to fasts'.

It is also lamentable that there have been some who have taken to fasting in order to offer immature help to mental patients. Whilst it can be stated, without hesitation, that there are forms of spiritual oppression and possession which required prolonged prayer with fasting, it must not be presumed that *prayer and fasting* are to be administered like medicine. For example, it is quite unscriptural, when confronted by a physiological depressive case, to order the *patient* to fast! Similarly, it is most improper to promise a recovery, to the family of a psychologically-unbalanced person, if they will undertake a prolonged fast on his behalf. In 1604, a legal canon was drawn up to cope with extremism of this kind, at the hand of such men as John Darrell, who would persist in such practices, despite obvious repeated failures. In the same way, only an extremist would copy the people of Nineveh and demand that *animals* should fast with the families, as a sign of sorrow (Jonah 3:7–8).

'Of all the means of grace, there is scarce any concerning which men have run into greater extremes, than that of religious fasting. How have some exalted this beyond all Scripture and reason; and others utterly disregarded it— as it were, revenging themselves by undervaluing as much as the former had over-valued it! Those have spoken of it as if it were all-in-all; if not the end itself, yet infallibly connected with it: these, as if it were just nothing; as if it were a fruitless labour, which had no relation at all thereto. Whereas it is certain the truth lies between them both. It is not all, nor yet is it nothing.'[14]

Although there is no doubt that fasting brings new vigour and fresh clarity of thought in its train, it is possible to carry forms of fasting to such an extreme that one is translated into realms which are not necessarily christian. There have been christians who have fasted for long periods, and who appear to have experienced moments of sheer bliss during the same, such as Daniel (see Daniel 9:20–21). On the other hand, heathen men have fasted for similar lengths of time and have recounted that they have known rapture of the soul also.

This is not likely to be a problem with those who abstain from meals for a period no longer than that advocated in this book, namely twenty-four hours. If, however, one is urged to extend the one-day discipline to a seven or fourteen days period *on the grounds that this will ensure rapturous blessing*, let him remember that this is not a scriptural teaching. Members of faiths which are anti-christian hold similar views and obtain these very results. To be caught up into a state of psychic bliss is not the same as entering the seventh heaven. It is not impossible, of course, for a present-day christian to have a Pauline experience of the world to come, but it is far from commonplace and *does not* happen to those who fast in order to ensure that it *does* take place. Extra-earthly experiences take place in the lives of believers only as a result of the grace of God; they cannot be realised—and remain divine—by any effort which *we* may exert.

The dangers mentioned above are the major ones, but there is still one more which breeds animosity and division in church life. This happens when spiritual pride is connected to false motives, producing a readiness to condemn others who do not appear to behave in the same way as the critic.

Spiritual pride is not far from any of us, and it is more common than most christians realise. It does not need many months to pass before the new recruit to fasting looks around at his fellow christians, and begins to make a comparison. It is very easy to allow oneself to think that the non-fasting christian is a veritable backslider and hopelessly incapable of being a recipient of blessing. The point to remember is *not* 'See how many acts of self denial I perform,' *but* 'My brother performs many acts of self-denial in secret, that I know nothing of'. The christian who bears in mind that his fellow believers are likely to be more disciplined than he is, despite any failings that he believes he can see, will be saved from thinking more highly of himself than he ought.

In every congregation there will be those who are unable to fast for medical reasons. To suggest that these people are disobeying God is outrageous. Also, every church will have at least one member who cannot fast, for psychological reasons. To taunt such a person about his need to fast is both cruel and anti-christian. We must remember that our hearts are established in the Faith by *grace* and not with food, and that when Paul saw personal condemnation causing havoc in one church, he wrote 'Let not him that eateth not, judge him that eateth'.[15]

Our personal motives are always important; this is particularly true with fasting. The people of God were once condemned for fasting for their own pleasure (Isaiah 58:3);

68

it would be sad if this could ever be said of us. 'If we keep a *holy* fast *unto the Lord*, we must be humbled in ourselves before the Lord. However, if—upon the confidence of our fasting—we become more sinful, with the idea that through obedience to Christ, in this one point, we may be disobedient in others; or, if the use of this discipline makes us rise against our brethren, and—after the example of the Pharisees—despise those who do not fast,[16] then fasting (which was appointed of the Lord to be our medicine) has become our poison.'[17]

NOTES

[1] J. Norval Geldenhuys: *Commentary on Luke:* note on Fasting: p. 198
[2] *Apologetics and Catholic Doctrine* by Michael Sheehan is typical
[3] A manual of church order, believed to have been compiled by the Apostles.
[4] *A Brief Discoverie of the False Church:* p. 89
[5] Charles Hodge: *Commentary on Second Corinthians:* p. 275
[6] Gordon Lindsay: *Prayer and Fasting:* p. 14
[7] R. V. G. Tasker: *Commentary on Matthew:* pp. 71–2
[8] Cunningham Giekie: *The Life and Words of Christ:* p. 401
[9] Part of Matthew Henry's comments on Matthew 6:16–18
[10] Part of Luther's comments on Matthew 6:16–18
[11] Matthew 23:1–4
[12] Phyllis Thompson: *D. E. Hoste:* p. 63
[13] J. Paterson Gledstone: *George Whitefield:* p. 193
[14] John Wesley: *Sermon on Fasting:* 22–Introduction–4
[15] Romans 14:3—This verse refers to the eating of cheap heathen ceremonial meat by christians, and the conscience problems which this creates, but the moral is the same.
[16] 1 Corinthians 8:8 and 13, Colossians 2:16. 1 Timothy 4:3, and Hebrews 9:10
[17] Thomas Cartwright: *The Holy Exercise of a True Fast*

V: The Times

'. . . and then shall they fast . . .'

Christians are tempted, sometimes, to excuse themselves from responsibility by stating that they have not been *led* to undertake it. This is permissible where the guidance of God is necessary, but it is inexcusable if the Bible has laid down firm principles upon the matter. The Almighty does not *guide* us to do what His Word plainly states to be His Will. God's Word requires not guidance but obedience. Therefore, if a mature christian says that although he reads his Bible regularly, and prays often, he has not ever been *led* to the conclusion that fasting is necessary, his reading must have been of a superficial kind. The saints of christian history have had quite the opposite reaction; they have read of the discipline and, without murmur, have begun to exercise it, as and when required.

We have looked at the words of our Lord 'when you fast' and have seen that they *presume* that a duty is involved. If we cling to the theory that, since these words *do not* constitute a *command*, there is no *duty* involved, then this chapter may be of little interest. Sufficient has been said on the subject of *command* and *duty* in the first chapter to state the historic case that the discipline of fasting is a duty which christians sometimes resort to. Therefore, we must now consider the all-important question of *when to do it*. Obedience, whilst accepting the clear command, can query the time of the order's fulfilment. If a soldier is told to accomplish a certain task by next week, he can both *take* his time and *choose* his time. However, if the command is more explicit, the day and the hour being stated, the soldier is not so free; he is bound by a clearly-defined order. Is fasting bound in such a way? Are there times and seasons for this discipline?

It would be easier for some people to adopt the practice of fasting if the Bible put the matter plainly in such words as, for example, 'Every christian shall abstain from food for the whole of Monday, every week'. Nevertheless, no other personal discipline is mentioned in this way. We are exhorted to assemble ourselves with other christians regularly,[1] we are told to set on one side a proportion of our earnings for God's work,[2] and we are commanded to do all in our power to maintain the unity of the Spirit[3] (to mention only three outward disciplines), but we are not given strict instructions, in the New Testament, regarding inward disciplines, such as—for example—prayer. Although it is true that the psalmist said 'Evening, and morning, and at noon, will I pray',[4] this was not a command, and Jesus did not suggest that this is what *we* should do. Therefore, whilst it may prove easier for some christians to fast if the Scriptures stated explicit times, this could be said of self-denial in every form. It is because no stated times are given that the discipline takes on a vital importance.

'If I make fasting an end in itself, something of which I say "Well now, because I have become a christian, I have to fast on such a day and at such a time in the year, because it is part of the christian religion", I might as well not do it. The special element in the act goes right out of it when that is done. This is something which is not peculiar to fasting. Can we not see exactly the same thing in the matter of prayer? It is a good thing for people, if they can, to have certain special times for prayer in their lives. But if I make up my programme for the day and say that at such and such an hour every day I must pray, and I just pray in order to keep to my programme, I am no longer praying. It is exactly the same with regard to the question of fasting.'[5]

71

Some have set out to regularise this discipline and to contain it within a Church programme. For example, the Book of Common Prayer[6] lists sixteen observable days for vigils, fasts, and abstinence; the Didache[7] ordered regular weekly fasts on both Wednesdays and Fridays; Roman Catholics decree that Friday must be observed as a day in which no meat is eaten; and the Carmelite, Carthusian and Cistercian Orders have laid down strict instructions concerning regular fasting. However, it must be obvious that any programme is bound to end up as formalistic as others have done, if it is applied to all christians in a legalistic way. So, although we have a measure of sympathy with the writers of the Didache in their attempt to lead christians away from heresy, one is forced to the conclusion that their comment 'let not your fasts be with hypocrites, for they fast on Mondays and Thursdays, but do you fast on Wednesdays and Fridays' is likely to lead to similar misunderstanding, in due course.

IN FASTINGS OFTEN

It must be concluded, therefore, that *individual* fasting is worthless if it becomes a ritual, and has no eternal benefit if it follows a routine. It must follow, then, that each believer is himself responsible for the way in which he fasts. There is no scriptural calendar to follow and no days and seasons to be observed.[8] Does this mean, that the individual christian should make some simple rules for himself? Shall he take part in his denomination's seasons of abstinence, such as Lent? Shall he eat to the full, every day, unless he is inwardly convinced that he should now desist? What policy shall he follow?

Since there are no rules, one could become lax without any difficulty; this appears to be the state in which the Church often finds itself. However, is it not true that because there are no rules, christians are free to fast *just as often* as they feel inclined to do? Freedom has different effects upon people, but to the follower of a disciplined Master, freedom does not mean licence, it means opportunity. We can fast on any day; there are no rules to *bind* us. We have every right to choose to miss the next meal, unless it is a public dinner, or one for which the preparations have been made already. A lack of rules, upon this matter, provides us with plenty of scope. For Paul, this meant that he could be in 'fastings often'.[9]

Although we have seen that fasting for a christian is not a ritual, and cannot be performed correctly if it is connected to a programme, some modern believers may find that they need to institute some system into their lives, at the beginning. There is no apparent harm in following such a course in order to experiment with the discipline, and in order to make life easier for the one who is in charge of household affairs. It is important, however, that even the simplest system is dropped as soon as one's eating habits are under control, in order that all links with ritual are broken. The aim is to be so disciplined that we can fast on any occasion, at short notice, whenever God calls us to it, or whenever a situation demands it.

A mature christian, who has no difficulty about missing meals, does not need to have an organised plan and may not need to have even a day of fasting every week; his fasting will be a personal matter between himself and his Lord and it will follow the pattern which his prayer life suggests to him is proper. However, some have found it sensible to fast for the whole of one day every week, in the way outlined in the next chapter, unless outside commitments and social functions do not permit it. Other christians have decided to follow other methods. Those who suffer from particular weaknesses of the body, as a result of warfare or hospital treatment, may find it difficult to go to these lengths, and it would be wrong to advise them

73

to do so. Since the New Testament does not lay down strict rules for us, it would be foolish to impose any scheme upon *every* believer, or to propose anything more drastic than one day per week.

SPECIAL SEASONS

In other words, if we are seeking an answer to the question 'When should a christian fast?', we have no biblical authority to think in terms of particular days in the week, or even dates in the year; we can only think in terms of heart-need. It is permissible for a young christian to adopt a personal programme in order to overcome the body's hunger habit, and to achieve the state in which his spirit rules over his appetite. Also, it is permissible for a local church, or a nation, to fix a date for a Fast Day, for a particular reason. However, the normal time for a mature christian to fast is when his heart tells him to do so. Jesus fasted, prior to the inauguration of His national ministry, because He was 'led of the Spirit';[10] this is the biblical pattern.

Grief over a church can cause a mature christian to forget food altogether, in the same way that personal disaster can make a hungry unbeliever declare that he 'can't eat'. Schism, cliques, heresy, and extremism have been known to bring pastors to their knees in fasting. If God has given a man a divine love for a congregation, that man suffers inwardly with every broken vow and every open sin; he is involved, in an integral way, with the total behaviour of his people. Ministers, for this reason, are—like Paul—in fastings often, if they serve churches in which there is deadness and apathy.

In churches where a Communion Service is held only once a quarter there are some grounds for suggesting that the worship might be preceded by, at least, a partial fast. This has been done in some circles and has done much to enhance the ceremonies for those participating. There is no warrant for insisting on this, however, and no biblical authority for stating that all Breaking of Bread worship should follow a fast. If anyone wishes to enforce such a ritual, he must turn to another authority than the Bible, as Roman Catholics know well.[11]

Sometimes, a church may consider it right to have a time of fasting prior to an important congregational event (Acts 13:1–3 and 14:23), and a married couple may be led, on occasions, to deny themselves personal pleasures (2 Samuel 11:11 and 1 Corinthians 7:5[12]). However, these seasons must be planned only as a result of a unanimous awareness of the Holy Spirit's leading. Enforced seasons of fasting against the wishes of the members of a congregation, or one married partner, lead to misunderstanding and division.

A Church would be foolish to adopt the advice of the Didache concerning baptism and fasting, for similar reasons. There is no biblical authority for stating that the person who is baptising should fast before the ceremony, and no spiritual wisdom in commanding the new convert to fast for two days before he is baptised.

In conclusion, it may be said that our Lord was more concerned about the *manner* in which christians fast, than the *time* of such fasting. This being the case, we may assume that our *motives* are more important than the *frequency* or *duration* of our fasting. However, there must be many believers who have been led to fast and yet have gone no further than the aroma of the next meal. For those who have always lived well, this is understandable, but their need for bodily discipline is obvious.

NOTES

[1] Hebrews 10:25
[2] 1 Corinthians 16:2
[3] Ephesians 4:3

4 Psalm 55:17

5 D. Martyn Lloyd-Jones: *Studies in the Sermon on the Mount:* vol. 2: p. 38

6 See the Tables in the *Book of Common Prayer*

7 A manual of church order, believed to have been compiled by the Apostles

8 Galatians 4:10

9 2 Corinthians 11:27

10 Matthew 4:1, Mark 1:12, and Luke 4:1

11 'The Church has decreed that to receive worthily, the subject must not only be in the state of grace, but must have fasted for three hours': Michael Sheehan: *Apologetics and Catholics Doctrine:* p. 185

12 Although the word 'fasting' does not appear in this verse, in the best N.T. documents, and so no teaching about fasting can be made from these words, the suggestion that self-denial may be practised in marriage, in the interests of prayer, is plain

VI: The Method

'...be not seen of men to fast...'

Having sought to establish that fasting is a duty which christians undertake on occasions, either when led of God, or when exhorted by church leaders, to do so, we now consider the practical issues. Although extremists have suggested that fasting requires no explanation, but simply practice, we turn now to the *method* of applying the discipline.

PREPARATION

In part of the Homily on Fasting, which is contained in number 35 of the Articles of the English Church, we find this advice: 'When men feel in themselves the heavy burden of sin, see damnation to be the reward of it, and behold, with the eye of their mind, the horror of hell, they tremble, they quake, and are inwardly touched with sorrowfulness of heart, and cannot but accuse themselves, and open their grief unto Almighty God, and call unto Him for mercy. This being done seriously, their mind is so occupied, partly with sorrow and heaviness, partly with an earnest desire to be delivered from this danger of hell and damnation, that *all desire of meat and drink* is laid apart, and loathsomeness of all wordly things and pleasure cometh in place.' If a christian is placed in that kind of spiritual situation, he will not need any advice on the necessary preparation for fasting; he will fast without any other preparation than that which the Holy Spirit gives to him. However, since many christians have fasted without being as deeply moved as this, although quite sure that they should fast, it is vital that the subject is considered properly.

Jesus said that we must not fast like 'the hypocrites, of a sad countenance; for they disfigure their faces, that they may be seen of men to fast' (Matthew 6:16). In other words, whilst there may be times when we shall be so full of sorrow that we cannot raise a smile, we are not to give the impression that we are sorrowful when we are not. In fact, Jesus said: 'When thou fastest, anoint thy head, and wash thy face; that thou be not seen of men to fast' (Matthew 6:17–18). We are to go right out of our way to make sure that when we are having a private fast (which in this respect is different, of course, from a corporate fast), we conceal this fact from as many people as possible. To do this we must look as *natural* as possible. We must not go to the foolish extreme of making ourselves look gay and frivolous, since this will only attract attention for different reasons than those just mentioned, but we must adopt the principles of camouflage. Those who dress solely in order to attract attention to themselves during a season of spiritual worship, only 'cover the hypocrisy of their hearts'.[1]

This means that although the Jews wore sackcloth, as a

sign of humility, when they fasted on their annual Day of Atonement, we must wear nothing to denote our secret action. They could dress themselves in this way because they were all involved in the national event. When there is a national Fast Day, one's clothes are unimportant; everyone is taking part and there is no secrecy. When individual christians fast in private, they must not appear to be undergoing any unusual experience. To wear special clothes, or to adopt a sad facial expression is to draw attention to the fact that some form of self-denial is in operation. Whether we draw attention to ourselves in order to impress others, the Lord, or our own selves (which is a very subtle sin), is not the point; to draw attention *at all* is, in our Master's opinion, quite improper. We may receive the praise of others by such measures, since every brand of superficial holiness earns earthly rewards, but it will not help the one who is fasting by one iota.

Jesus said that if we fast in such a way that all and sundry are aware of it we shall 'receive our reward'. He was referring to the praise which people bestow ignorantly upon those who have an appearance of holiness. If we are so disciplined that we can fast without pain, but are still so full of pride that we must flaunt our acts of self-denial before everyone we meet, there is no more reward for us than that which is then given. Any reward for such behaviour is limited to that kind which people are able to donate freely, at the time.

Our motive is, therefore, of the utmost importance to our preparation for fasting. We should not think it a waste of time to examine our hearts and ask ourselves why we are taking this step. If it is for any reason other than for the glory of God, we may as well save ourselves the trouble of the discipline. 'Let our intention herein be this, and this alone, to glorify our Father which is in heaven; to express our sorrow and shame for our manifold transgressions of

His holy law; to wait for an increase of purifying grace, drawing our affections to things above; to add seriousness and earnestness to our prayers; to avert the wrath of God; and to obtain all the great and precious promises which He hath made to us in Jesus Christ.'[2]

LOCATION

When our Lord taught His disciples the manner of private christian prayer, He advised them to retire to their own rooms, alone and apart (Matthew 6:6); seasons of personal prayer require privacy. However, when He instructed the same disciples about fasting there was no mention of separation either from the world or from other christians; this form of self-denial does not demand privacy.

If all fasting took place in the privacy of an inner room, christians would be gravely limited and would be out of communication with family, church, and business; this state of affairs would create impossible situations. It is because christian fasting must take place during the ordinary routine of life that Jesus emphasised the need to behave in such a way that we 'be not seen of men to fast'. If we act in a normal way, following the usual patterns of behaviour, we shall be seen only by the Father; our fasting will be 'in secret', although it will not be 'in private'.

This means that when a working man sets apart a day, in the middle of the week, on which to fast, it need not necessarily be spent in prayer. He cannot both earn his living and be upon his knees; he can live in a spirit of prayer, but he cannot pray openly. However, he can *fast* and this is a part of the man's worship and devotion. Some have suggested that it is useless to fast without prayer. It is pointless to fast without a spirit of worship and love for God, but there is no doubt that a christian can fast correctly and also be at work, if he is called to do this. Jesus made no reference about fasting only on the Lord's Day, or when one is not working. The Jewish Day of Atonement Fast was a national event, and it was quite in keeping that they ceased from their labours, as well as from food.

It should be emphasised, however, that fasting cannot be separated easily from prayer; the two go together. A praying christian should fast sometimes, and a christian who declares that he believes in fasting should be regular in his times of prayer. A christian who fasts regularly, but hardly ever prays, is either in danger of becoming a fanatic, or else not a *christian*—in the way that the Bible understands the meaning of that word.

If someone feels led of God to devote a day or more to personal fellowship with Christ in fasting, he must spend the time in prayer and devotional reading. To fast only, for so long, and do no other spiritual exercises, is of no christian value. On a national day of fasting, there must be prayer, and when a congregation gives up a Sunday to fasting, the whole time should be full of prayer and praise. This is so obvious from the many texts already quoted in connection with *watchings* and *fast days*, that there is little need to repeat the facts here. On the other hand, it would be wrong for us to be so bound up by this truth that we become unable to accept a situation in which a believer both works and fasts.

We have seen in the first chapter that the normal period of a christian fast is one whole day, involving the missing of three meals, at least. There is abundant evidence that this was the usual period for the fasts recorded in both the Old and New Testaments. If a nation calls its people to observe a fast, we may expect that this will be for one day only. Similarly, if a church is led of God to fast, for a particular reason, the time specified is usually for one day only. A fast of one day's duration is the normal fast, and should not be exceeded unless one is called to do so.

However, we must agree that this period has been extended on more than one occasion. For example, when Esther announced her special fast, she declared that it was to be for *three* days and nights (Esther 4:16), when David's valiant men mourned the loss of Saul and his sons, they fasted for *seven* days (1 Chronicles 10:12), and when Daniel realised the significance of a vision, he continued a partial fast for three weeks (Daniel 10:2–3). It is possible that we may intend to fast for one day, but not be able to return to eating for several days, in the same way that prayer cannot always be drawn to a close at the time expected. So then, although we have seen that biblical fasts are usually for only twenty-four hours, we must acknowledge that this period is not an ordinance.

Unusual fasts, of up to forty days in length, have not been common, but have taken place often enough for us to realise that God may call someone to this experience, if necessary. Moses was without both food and water for forty days[3] (Exodus 34:28 and Deuteronomy 9:9); Elijah went in the strength of one meal for forty days (1 Kings 19:8; and Jesus stayed in the wilderness, without food, for forty days (Matthew 4:2, Mark 1:13, and Luke 4:2). It is well within the bounds of possibility for a healthy person to fast for such a period today, as long as sufficient rest is taken and the correct amount of water drunk. Many non-christian people have denied themselves food, for a similar length of time, simply in order to improve their health. The experience is not so awful as some may imagine. However, it would be incorrect to state that a long fast is either expected of christians, or spiritually beneficial to them, of necessity.

When Paul realised how much he had persecuted the Lord, he was unable to eat for three days (Acts 9:9); his fasting was not undertaken with any pre-conceived motive —he abstained without realising it. On a journey into Galilee, Jesus sat down by the side of the well near Sychar; He was very weary, thirsty, and hungry. Yet, when the disciples returned from their errand, in search of a meal, Jesus had no interest in food any more. His concern for the lost soul of the misguided woman, made eating an unimportant pastime. His fasting, though real to the disciples, who were amazed by it, was the result of his preoccupation with the work to which He had been called. That his behaviour caused him to be misunderstood was of no importance (John 4:32). Paul informed the christians at Philippi that he had learned the secret of contentment, in every situation: 'I know both how to be abased and how to abound ... how to be full and to be hungry' (Philippians 4:12), clearly speaking from considerable experience. The five thousand followers, and their families, who were so intent on Christ's preaching that they lost all sense of time, had to be reminded that they were due for a meal (Matthew 15:32 and Mark 8:1–4).

The above incidents refer to anorexia (a lack of general desire for food), but which may be termed fasting since it happened in the context of religious experiences, although not entered into voluntarily. These instances were not caused by spiritual mourning, and were not in response to the call of God, and yet the fasting was genuine and true to christian experience. Such experiences were quite different from the involuntary fast of the lost Egyptian soldier in 1 Samuel 30:11–13, the enforced hunger of the besieged citizens in 2 Kings 25:3, and the unconcern for food of the worried sailors in Acts 27:33. Every active christian worker knows something of involuntary fasting, and the remarkable way in which one is sustained during these unexpected events. We cannot prepare for them, and have no sense of need during them.

Modern advertising, in Western countries, has encouraged the idea that munching snacks, between meals, is both desirable and envigorating; the idea is not upheld by dieticians, and is condemned by dentists. Considering that the average person, in the Western hemisphere, has three meals each day, the need for snacks between meals is not obvious. Neither is it easy to see why anyone should need any food during the period of twelve hours prior to 'breakfast'. These innovations may be connected to the general indiscipline of many in these days. However, for christians, there should be a disciplined approach to eating, as to all other departments of life.

If any biblical character contributed anything to the subject of dietary temperance it was John the Baptist. From all accounts (Matthew 3:4 and 11:18, Mark 1:6, Luke 1:15 and 7:33), he did not touch one drop of either fresh fruit juice or fermented wine, in the whole of his life, and adhered to a strict diet of wild insects and honey. This behaviour may be regarded as unusual and unique, but the example is worth considering. Is it not possible that some of the spiritual weakness of many modern churches is due, in part, at least, to a lack of temperance in the realm of eating? Is it possible to be above smoking, gambling, drug addiction, and alcoholism, but to be intemperate as far as diet is concerned?

Daniel saw fit to eat the plainest of food for ten days (Daniel 1:8–20) rather than 'defile himself with the king's meat', and profited by doing so. All temperance is both spiritually and physically beneficial, and so we may be assured that dietary temperance is also.

A normal fast of only twenty-four hours' duration needs no special equipment or diet sheet; one needs only to stop eating altogether, and to drink warm water when one would normally drink tea, coffee, or something else. Those who have not fasted previously, may find it helpful to drink warm water sweetened with honey, at the beginning. Also, those who dare not undertake so drastic a discipline, for fear of the consequences, may eat an orange in place of the usual meals, for the first few times, in order to prove that this abstinence is not deadly. Although it is possible to fast without water for a whole day, this is not advised in general.

A fast of two or three days can be attempted, on the basis of the above information, without any fear, as long as warm water is taken at intervals of no less than four hours.

Fasting for longer than one whole day is not the general rule of the biblical discipline, but a christian may be called to continue for up to three days; there is no harm in this, if the advice given is followed closely. To fast for longer than three days, and to continue for as many as forty days, raises the question of bodily evacuation and the need for a warm water enema at least every other day. Although we may assume that Moses and Elijah were not acquainted with the enema method of inner cleansing, they did not eat modern foodstuffs, which can tend to clog the human body, and may harm the intestines if not evacuated frequently. If the one who is fasting has been eating only natural food during the week prior to a long fast, he may not find bodily elimination necessary. However, an enema has the effect of washing internally, as well as assisting evacuation, and so has beneficial advantages.

It is possible to fast for long periods, and continue at work, by eating only one orange (or, at the most, two) at each normal mealtime. This simple partial fast is the one advocated by Nature Cure specialists for those suffering from many internal disorders and overweight problems. With this fruit diet, warm water drinks (or pearl barley water[4]) must be taken also. Most people have no trouble with an orange diet despite the idea that it must be over-acidic. However, for some, it may prove better to begin the day with a glass of hot lemon water which has been sweetened with honey. It should be borne in mind that only fresh fruit should be used in the preparation of this fruit diet; tinned fruit and juices are not suitable, and neither is unripe fruit.

No person living on drugs, or taking pills, should consider a fast unless given permission to do so. Even as the suffering are excused, so must those who live by prescriptions. Whilst it could be true that a few days of fasting may help someone who is ill because of an improper diet, advice should be obtained from the practitioner responsible. As we have seen earlier, fasting is beneficial to christians, but unhealthy people are not able to undertake this discipline either as fully, or for as long, as healthy ones.

NOTES

[1] From Matthew Poole's comments on Matthew 6:16–18

[2] John Wesley: *Sermon on Fasting:* 22–4–1

[3] There is a suggestion in Deuteronomy 9:18 that this was an eighty day fast altogether

[4] Pearl Barley water is made by dropping one tablespoonful of pearl barley into one pint of water. The water is brought to the boil and then taken off the barley and ejected. A fresh pint of water is now added to the pearl barley, together with the juice of a lemon quarter and two teaspoonfuls of honey. This is brought back to the boil and allowed to simmer for 15 minutes. After cooling, and straining, the water is ready

VII: The Opposition

'... my knees are weak through fasting ...'

There is an equal and opposite reaction to every action, in all spheres of life, and so those who fast must expect that there will be adverse conditions to face. The Bible does not give us much information along these lines, since this is the practical outcome of a spiritual undertaking. As soon as a christian involves himself in any spiritual matter, he finds that there is opposition.

HUNGER FEELINGS

Someone has said that all feelings are unreliable in christian experience. One could debate the truth of this statement, but it has been noted that the senses of our body —which are so useful at other times—can be a nuisance to us if we are seeking to do something purely spiritual. We are not very aware of our body, unless we are ill, even though our senses are real; but there is no doubt that by the time one has missed two meals, a feeling of 'emptiness' will have spread through the body. In fact, we may be tempted to think that we are in the process of starving to death! It will take much more than missing two meals to starve a healthy person, and the initial awareness of hunger, though very real, is only a *habit* feeling which has been acquired over the years. The body has a routine, and it does not take easily to a break in that routine—any more than our pets would. Our bodies come to assume that food will arrive at regular intervals.

If this habit feeling is ignored it will leave eventually; it is only a feeling. It is bound to appear, and we can't stop it coming, because habits do die hard. One must fast many times before this feeling does *not* manifest itself. So, therefore, anyone who fasts may as well assume that he will have this feeling and that he will have to regard it as opposition. If a glass of warm water is taken at intervals of not less than every four hours, the feeling of hunger will be diminished considerably.

Those who fast for long periods will discover that they lose all sense of wanting food, after several days, but that a genuine hunger returns to them when the body is truly in need of nourishment once more.

WEAKNESS

Physical weakness will not trouble everyone, but if one fasts for *more* than three meals, this symptom will appear. If meals are missed for not more than one day a week, as suggested, weakness will not be of much concern. However, if someone decides to devote two days of holiday to fasting and prayer, he will discover that he has become quite weak. He will feel as though he can do little more than lie down or sit; walking any distance may be impossible after three days of fasting. In fact, until we have become experienced at missing food, for two or three days at a time, we shall be unable to avoid this feeling of weakness.

When Saul heard that the Philistines were likely to win the battle, on the following day, he stopped eating and gave himself to ardent prayer (1 Samuel 28:19-25); this made him so lacking in strength that his handmaid was anxious for his life. And when the Psalmist fasted, he wrote that his knees were weak (Psalm 109:24). However, practice makes perfect with this discipline, as with other things, and so those who abstain at frequent intervals become unaware of the weakness, in due course.

If one continues a fast for more than four days, he is likely to find that considerable strength comes to him eventually, despite the lack of sustenance; the promise that 'they that wait upon the Lord shall renew their strength', comes true in these circumstances.

87

Headaches are reaction pains in the body which inform us that something is wrong. Usually, they serve a useful function and are invaluable to both patient and practitioner. When someone fasts, there must be a headache, for the first few times, as the body reacts to the new situation and seeks to overcome it by natural means. It is unwise to take aspirin in order to deaden the pain, which is not severe. The headache should be ignored until it passes, which will be when the body has accepted the situation. If the headache is severe and does not pass, there are good grounds for seeking advice from a doctor.

When John Wesley decided that he was doing himself no good by drinking strong tea, he banished it from his diet completely, overnight, instead of diluting the brew over a period. As a result, he had severe headaches for two days. However, when his body became acquainted with the new arrangement, the headaches disappeared.

BAD BREATH

Young people, especially girls, are very conscious of bad breath. Unfortunately this is one possible symptom of fasting. It is caused by the coating which appears on the upper surface of the tongue, soon after the commencement of a fast. The body, on the look-out for food, begins to digest such waste material, and deposits of fat, as are available to it. The coating on the tongue is not harmful and should not be removed by brushing; it is the outward proof that inner elimination is in progress. As soon as the digestive organs have been purified, the breath returns to normal.

The best way to cope with this form of opposition is to be armed with a glass of fresh natural lemon juice which has been sweetened only with honey. It is not advisable to rely on the kind of tablets which are on sale for ordinary bad breath.

PERSECUTION

The most embarrassing opposition of all is deliberate persecution by those christians who refuse to agree that fasting is a discipline for today, and so go out of their way to make things difficult for those who wish to practise his discipline. This should be anticipated in days when apathy is rampant, and indiscipline is an accepted way of life. Such opposition must be considered, and treated, in the same way that christians approach all other forms of persecution; a gracious spirit of quietness will succeed where other methods fail.

Let it not be thought that, since fasting is a desirable thing, eating is a sin. This would be the conclusion of a fanatical extremist. The Bible has as much to say about the pleasure of consuming good food, as it declares about fasting. For example, 'That which I have seen to be good and to be comely is for one to eat and to drink';[1] 'Into whatsoever house you shall enter . . . remain, eating and drinking such things as they give';[2] 'And day by day, continuing stedfastly with one accord in the temple, and breaking bread at home, they did take their food with gladness and singleness of heart.'[3]

There is a time and a place for both joyous eating and sorrowful fasting; neither should be forgotten; neither should be exalted.

NOTES

[1] Ecclesiastes 5:18
[2] Luke 10:5–7
[3] Acts 2:46

Bibliography

ADDISON, Berkely, and others: *Lent Lectures:* London: 1859.

AIKIN, J.: *Food for National Penitence:* London: 1793.

ALEXANDER, J. A.: *Commentary on Mark:* Banner of Truth: 1960.

ASAPH, the Bishop of St.: *The National Fast:* London: 1847.

BARKER, P. R. P.: *Chambers's Encyclopaedia:* George Newnes: 1963.

BARROW, Henry: *A Brief Discoverie of the False Church.* Dort: 1590.

BIRCHER, Ruth: *Eating Your Way to Health:* Faber and Faber: 1961.

BLUNT, J. J.: *History of the Christian Church:* John Murray: 1861.

BONAR, Andrew: *Leviticus:* Banner of Truth: 1966.

BOUNDS, E. M.: *Power Through Prayer:* Oliphants: 1958.

BOURNE, F. W.: *Billy Bray:* Epworth Press: 1937.

BROWN, John: *Discourses and Sayings of our Lord:* Banner: 1967.

BUCHINGER, Otto H. F.: *About Fasting:* Thorsons: 1961.

BURNS, James: *Revivals—Their Laws and Leaders:* Hodder: 1909.

CARTWRIGHT, Thomas: *The Holy Exercise of a True Fast.* London: 1610.

CARTWRIGHT, Thomas: *A Treatise of Christian Religion* London: 1597.

CLARK, Blake: *'Fasting':* Article in *The Reader's Digest* March 1963.

COLLINSON, Patrick: *Elizabethan Puritan Movement:* Cape: 1967.

CONNELL, J. Clement: *'Fasting':* Article in *The Christian* 13-3-64.

CROSS, F. L.: *The Oxford Dictionary of the Christian Church* Oxford University Press: 1958.

EDWARDS, Jonathan: *The Life of David Brainerd:* Marshall & Simpkin: 1818.

EDWARDS, Jonathan: *Select Works:* Banner of Truth: 1958.

EUSEBIUS, Bishop of Caesarea: *An Ecclesiastical History* Bagster: 1842.

FARRAR, F. W.: *The Early Days of Christianity:* Cassell: 1882

FINNEY, Charles G.: *Lectures on Revivals:* Oliphants: 1928.

FROGGATT, S.: *The Churchman's A.B.C.:* James Nisbet: 1900

GAINSBURGH, A.: *The Fast Day:* London: 1832.

GEIKIE, Cunningham: *The Life and Words of Christ:* Cassell 1887.

GELDENHUYS, J. Norval: *Commentary on Luke:* Wm. B Eerdmans : 1950.

GODET, F.: *Commentary on Luke:* T. & T. Clark: 1887.

GRUBB, Norman: *Rees Howells—Intercessor:* C.L.C. : 1956.

GUNNING, Bishop of Ely: *The Holy Fast:* London: 1677.
HENDRIKSEN, William: *Commentary on John:* Banner of Truth: 1959.
HENRY, Matthew: *Commentary on the Bible:* Wm. MacKenzie: 1721.
HODGE, Charles: *Princeton Sermons:* Banner of Truth: 1958.
HODGE, Charles: *Commentary on Second Corinthians:* Banner: 1963.
HUNT, Bruce F.: *For A Testimony:* Banner of Truth: 1966.
KNOX, John: *Order and Doctrine of a General Fast:* Edinburgh: 1565.
LINDSAY, Gordon: *Prayer and Fasting:* Dallas, Texas: 1957.
LLOYD-JONES, D. Martyn: *Studies in the Sermon on the Mount:* Inter Varsity Press: 1960.
LUTHER, Martin: *Works: Vol. 21: Sermon on the Mount:* Concordia: 1956.
LUTHER, Martin: *Works: Vol. 48: Letters:* Fortress Press: 1963.
MACLEAN, A. J.: *Liturgy and Worship:* London: 1932.
MICHELET, M.: *The Life of Luther:* G. Bell and Sons: 1911.
MORTON WHITBY, H. A.: *Preservation of Health:* Thorsons: 1967.
MOSHEIM, John L.: *An Ecclesiastical History: vol. 2:* Baynes: London: 1825.
PALMER, W.: *Christian Doctrine and Practice:* under Fasting: Burns: 1841.
PATTISON, M. W. D.: *The Life Story of Paget Wilkes:* Oliphants: 1938.
PEAKE, Arthur S.: *Commentary on the Bible:* Nelson: 1919.
PEPYS, Samuel: *The Diary of Samuel Pepys:* Macmillan: 1925.
POOLE, Matthew: *Commentary on the Holy Bible:* Banner: 1963.
PRESBYTER A.: *Fasting Briefly Considered:* London: 1853.
SALISBURY A.: *The National Fast:* London: 1854.
SAVAGE, John: *'Fasting':* Article in *The Life of Faith:* 9–3–67.
SHEEHAN, Michael: *Apologetics and Catholic Doctrine:* M. H. Gill: 1962.
STALEY, V.: *The Fasting Days Appointed:* London: 1899.
TASKER, R. V. G.: *Commentary on Matthew:* Inter Varsity Press: 1961.
THOMPSON, Phyllis: *D. E. Hoste:* China Inland Mission: 1947.
THORNWELL, J. H.: *Fast Day Sermons:* Rudd & Carleton: 1861.
UNGER, Merrill F.: *Bible Dictionary:* Moody Press: 1957.
URWICK, William: *Nonconformity in Hertfordshire:* Hazell, Watson and Viney: 1884.
VINE, W. E.: *Commentary on Isaiah:* Oliphants: 1965.
WESLEY, John: *Sermons on Several Occasions:* Epworth Press: 1944.
ANONYMOUS: *What is Fasting:* Seeley, Jackson & Halliday: London: 1855.

General Index

93

Scriptural Index